TRACING YOUR TWENTIETH-CENTURY ANCESTORS

D0891118

FAMILY HISTORY FROM PEN & SWORD

TRACING YOUR TWENTIETH-CENTURY ANCESTORS

A Guide for Family Historians

Karen Bali

Pen & Sword
FAMILY HISTORY

First published in Great Britain in 2016
PEN & SWORD FAMILY HISTORY
an imprint of
Pen & Sword Books Ltd
47 Church Street,
Barnsley
South Yorkshire,
S70 2AS

ISBN 978 178383 103 6

Typeset in Palatino by CHIC GRAPHICS

Printed and bound in England by
CPI Group (UK), Croydon, CR0 4YY

Pen & Sword Books Ltd incorporates the imprints of Pen & Sword
Archaeology, Atlas, Aviation, Battleground, Discovery, Family History,
History, Maritime, Military, Naval, Politics, Railways, Select, Social History,
Transport, True Crime, Claymore Press, Frontline Books, Leo Cooper,
Praetorian Press, Remember When, Seaforth Publishing and Wharncliffe.

For a complete list of Pen & Sword titles please contact
PEN & SWORD BOOKS LTD
47 Church Street, Barnsley, South Yorkshire, S70 2AS, England
E-mail: enquiries@pen-and-sword.co.uk
Website: www.pen-and-sword.co.uk

CONTENTS

ACKNOWLEDGEMENTS

There are several people to thank who have helped to make this project possible. Friends Barbara Allen, Nicky Lockyer and Anna Seabourne, for their support and practical help, Simon Hall, for his encouragement, and Neil MacFarlane for turning things around when it seemed impossible. As always, my greatest gratitude is to Sunil, my wonderful husband of twenty-five years, to whom this book is dedicated.

Author's note: some names have been changed in the case histories to protect the privacy of the individuals featured.

* * *

Cover photographs:

Young soldier – Edward A.F. Newman, *c.* 1914 (with thanks to Anthony Richmond)
Policeman – H. George Grant, *c.* 1950 (with thanks to Ellen Collier)
Memorial – Nunhead Cemetery Scout Memorial (with thanks to Alan Patient, www.plaquesoflondon.co.uk)

INTRODUCTION

When the subject of genealogy comes up, the focus is often on 'how far back' someone has managed to trace their family. We may boast about ancestors deep in the past, quote dates and events from long ago and have documentary evidence with pedigree lines from 1690, but focusing on our roots is only half the story. Yes, families have roots and history but the past is not the only dimension; there are also branches and leaves – the recent past, the present and the future.

Early on in my research career I chose to focus on modern records and tracing living relatives. To me, there is little point in knowing minute details about the lives of distant, long-dead ancestors, if you have no interest in your grandparents' generation or if you have only a superficial relationship with your aunts, uncles and cousins – living, breathing kin who share your heritage and DNA. It follows that it can enrich and expand our research to learn more about the lives of relatives in our living memory, the faces in our photo albums, the people who influenced and shaped our parents, and therefore us.

The obsession with 'getting back' means that recent generations are mostly overlooked. Perhaps this is because the past that we remember, or that our parents talked about, just doesn't seem interesting or different enough from the present we live in today. To the next generation and their descendants, however, your recent past is their history, one that may absorb and fascinate them as much as the lives of distant ancestors do for so many of us today. Researching and recording your twentieth-century ancestors can be your eternal legacy to them.

Before you Start

If your mission is to work backwards as far into the distant past as possible, you might probably start with the earliest known records about your ancestors and take it from there. If you want to examine the recent past, however, the methodology is a little different.

Firstly, I suggest that you gather all of the documents that you have relating to your family, even ones that you have looked at before, if you think you know everything that's on them or you don't think there will be any information that will help you. Take your birth certificate, for example. Note not just your name and where you were born but items like who registered your birth (most likely one of your parents), the address where they lived (is it a house that you know?), and the occupation of your father. Examine birth, marriage and death certificates, wills, diaries and family bibles in detail, again noting all the information that you know, didn't know or thought you knew. Next, move on to your photograph album, writing names, dates, places and events on the back. (It is helpful to write the details on a label first, before sticking it to the back of the photo, so as not to damage the picture.) Apart from checking and discovering information, you're filling in gaps and recording things that you might know now but might not be able to recall in a couple of decades.

The human memory is a strange and wonderful thing but it is flawed and it can also be fragile. In a box file with my primary school reports and a couple of school books I have a class photograph from one of my early years at primary school around 1971. Our small group is outside a school building that I remember so well. The headmaster stands on one side, looking serious and a little stern; it is summer so the children are all in short sleeves and dresses, some squinting in the sunshine. There are twenty-nine children, which at my small village school made up not just the class but the whole year (we had three classes – the lower, the middle and the top, and the whole school had only around sixty-five pupils). When I moved out of the family home around the age of 21, I looked at this photograph and reeled off the names of the teachers and all the pupils (first names and surnames) with no problem at all. A couple of years later, when I moved house and looked at the photo again, one or two names eluded me. Luckily, at that point I wrote the names I could recall on the back of the photo and was able to find out from an old school friend the names of all the others. I forgot about this picture for several years, as work, marriage and children became my priorities for a while, but it resurfaced around five years ago while I was searching my loft for school certificates. Purposely without looking at the back, I examined the images of everyone in the picture and tried to remember who they were. I remembered the teachers, the two or three friends I played with and a couple of children who lived near me. For some I recalled first names but not surnames, for others it was the opposite way around. However, although I recalled the faces, I was horrified to realise I did not remember the names of around a third of the class at all. I was only in my forties and I'd had no illnesses or injuries that would have affected my memory but still, with the passing of time, the names of these children I had seen almost every day for the first six years of my education had disappeared from my mind. Refusing to give in and check the back, I stared at this photo several times for a couple of minutes every day over the next week or so, reliving lessons, playtimes and school trips and imagining these children in that village school setting. To my relief, some of the forgotten names gradually started coming back to me. On occasions I dreamed about my school days and one of the elusive names would come to mind when I woke up; sometimes names popped into my head while I was doing mundane things like driving, cooking or hanging washing on the line. After a couple of weeks I had almost a full house and then felt no shame in turning the photo over to check. The names of my classmates that were initially missing had been filed in my brain's version of the recycle bin – no longer used, not needed and taking some effort to restore but most of them were there and intact, although a couple were lost or corrupted.

This exercise was a lesson to me – memory alone cannot be trusted and it is important to record as much as possible as soon as possible, lest it be lost for ever. This isn't just important for me and for you but for our relatives who hold facts and memories inside their heads which need to be 'downloaded' while they are still around and have the capacity to pass these things on.

This brings us to the next task of speaking to relatives, something that it is important to do as soon as possible. 'One day' often never comes and even with the best of intentions it can be difficult to find time and space to spend some time with relatives who will not always be with us.

Case History

Russell recounts the experience of missing out on one last phone conversation with his mother. 'It was during the 1980s and I worked as a technician for a national company, driving a van and visiting customers,' he recalls. 'To save money on my home phone bills I used to call my mother about once a week from the office when I checked in at the end of the day, at which time it was usually quiet. One day I arrived back at base, the boss had gone home and the office was empty. I hadn't spoken to my mother for a couple of weeks, and had been meaning to ask her a couple of things about family but kept forgetting. As I picked up the phone and started dialling the number I remembered that I had a badminton match that evening so I put the phone down, thinking that I would call her the next day. She died suddenly later that night and I lost the opportunity for ever to ask her those questions. It has taken a long time to get over my regret, and the realisation that there were things she knew that she can now never tell me.'

Having heard people say countless times that they wish they had asked their now-deceased parents or grandparents questions while they had the opportunity, I would urge anyone not to put it off any longer – fix a date, arrange a family reunion, go and visit, make the most of family events like weddings, birthdays, anniversaries and even funerals, and get talking about the family.

An Illegitimate Grandfather

Forbes had always been led to believe that his paternal grandfather, after whom he was named, was a foundling, abandoned on the steps of a public building in Aberdeen before being taken in and adopted by a kind family. He mentioned to his mother at a family gathering that he would very much like to get a kilt to wear to a wedding but didn't know which tartan to order – the clan of his family surname was not his by heritage as this was the name of the family that raised his grandfather. His mother 'let slip' that actually she did know who her father-in-law's mother was but it had been 'kept quiet'. Forbes questioned her gently then went away and wrote down what she had told him. His mother had given only the briefest of details but it was enough for Forbes to obtain his grandfather's birth certificate. It transpired that his great-grandmother, Elizabeth Laing, was a maid at Balmoral and that the family who raised her illegitimate son were friends of her father. He was able to discover much more about his grandfather's life, his adoptive family and his biological ancestry. He also got his kilt.

When you do have an opportunity for a conversation with older relatives about the past, don't just talk but listen. Hearing and listening, as anyone who has undergone counselling training understands, are two very different things. Really listening takes effort, time and concentration. Interviewing older relatives requires a degree of planning, patience, checking, reflecting and complete focus and it should not be rushed. When it comes to subjects that some relatives might find difficult, shameful or awkward, be gentle and understanding but offer the point that this information might be important to future generations. 'Let sleeping dogs lie' was the attitude cultivated in many families and there are often 'things that are not mentioned'. Matters such as suicide, illegitimacy, abandonment, adultery, imprisonment and bigamy were often not just swept under the carpet but locked in boxes and buried so deep that they are tremendously difficult even to recall, much less to talk about. If there are people, events and circumstances that really are too painful or embarrassing for your relatives to tell you, one suggestion is that you invite them to write it down, seal it in an envelope and leave it with their papers to be opened after their death.

When it comes to recording what is said, there are several options. A good, old-fashioned notebook and pen is one way. I would suggest using a bound notebook, preferably with acid-free paper, rather than an exercise book or reporter's notebook, as it is sturdier, more durable and less likely to lose pages. Record the dates and places that conversations took place. If you want to make a sound recording or video, ensure that you check with your interviewee that they are comfortable with this, although most people forget it is happening once they start talking. Also, remember to take a digital camera or portable scanner to take copies of documents and photographs. All of this might take time and effort to organise and execute, but you will be glad that you did and future generations will thank you for it. (There will be more about using technology to preserve the results of your research in Chapter 12.)

A Book for his Children

Frank decided to pay for a service that provided him with bound books that he could leave for his children. He was a printer by trade after taking an apprenticeship in the 1950s and working in Fleet Street for more than twenty-five years. Frank had been raised by his father and grandmother after his mother abandoned the family when he was a few weeks old. He hired a researcher to discover what had happened to his mother, eventually finding out that she had remarried and had three more children. One thing led to another and he found out lots more about his ancestors on both sides. For example, his strict, Catholic, 'widowed' grandmother was a single woman who invented a husband and had two illegitimate sons. He also had Irish ancestors with descendants now all over the world. All of the research results and document copies were kept in a folder but he wanted something more permanent. He set about writing out his story in longhand, then had it checked, edited and typed up. This manuscript, together with the documents and some family photographs, was sent off to a printer to be made into a hardback book with a photo of him and his late wife on the cover. Frank was thrilled with the five copies that came back; he gave one to each of his children and kept a couple for himself. He says that it was well worth the expense to have his story preserved for future generations.

Data Protection

One of the challenges of researching our recent history is the issue of privacy. With some records, such as the census, there is a statutory closure period with no negotiation (more about that in Chapter 2) but with many records and resources the conditions for access are more ambiguous.

'Data Protection' is sometimes quoted as a reason for withholding access to records but it's far from simple; the legislation is complex, lengthy and difficult to interpret. The rules relate to the collection, processing, storage, disclosure and disposal of information that is considered to be personal. There is a thirty-page document from the Information Commissioner's Office entitled 'Determining what is personal data' – and if it is this complicated for staff making decisions about access, then the layman has little chance when challenging a refusal.

Broadly, if information relates to the individual making the application for records held about them, then access must be allowed or copies of documents supplied, unless there is a serious and valid reason (such as the prevention of crime). Data protection only applies to information about living persons (hence probate records are publicly available after the distribution of an estate). Also, information should be accessible if it has already been in the public domain (such as newspaper reports) or where permission for sharing has been granted. If access to records is refused it is worth challenging the decision and asking for a review as sometimes the rules do not actually apply to the records that we want to use for our research.

To find out more and view the principles of the Data Protection Act, visit the website of the Information Commissioner's Office at https://ico.org.uk.

Data protection should not be confused with Freedom of Information, which relates to the right to access information on the activities of public authorities.

Online sources

Much of the information that is used for research today is accessed online, either on the internet, via subscription and pay-per-view websites or from indexed digital images.

Whilst a great deal of information is free, there are charges for some of the most useful resources that are used for family research. This is understandable, considering the time and cost of making these records available, but it does mean that the cost of your research can add up over time. Family history is a hobby like any other and it is helpful to budget for it; it is easy to get carried away downloading records and ordering documents meaning that the expenses can mount up. Some public libraries, local history centres and archives offer free access to pay-per-view websites such as Ancestry and Find My Past, so it is worth planning to spend some time researching there in order to take advantage of this.

It's helpful to remember that to make these millions of records searchable, they first must be indexed. Indexing from original records requires skill, knowledge and patience but it is a mundane job that is often done either by volunteers or by people with little understanding of the records they are indexing. In addition, most of the original records were handwritten and in a style of writing that is sometimes difficult to interpret. Therefore, even the best indexes contain at least some errors and omissions. Soundex and phonetic searches might go some way to locating index entries that are incorrect, but certain searches may require some lateral thinking in terms of alternative spellings, or browsing of the original documents to find information relating to your ancestors.

I very much welcome constructive feedback, particularly about information that is out of date, omitted or incorrect, so that future editions and other work can be as accurate as possible. Please do contact me through my website at www.people-search.co.uk.

Chapter 1

LIFE IN THE TWENTIETH CENTURY

The twentieth century is the century in which most readers of this book were born, unless coming to family research early. At the time of writing (summer 2015), the last couple of decades of the 1900s feel like yesterday. Like many people, I remember free school milk, the miners' strike, the first moon landing and the queen's Silver Jubilee; I also remember the days of red phone boxes, black and white TV and deliveries from the milkman, coalman and baker.

So before we explore the records, resources and research methods that can help bring our recent past to life, let's explore the twentieth century, remind ourselves of some key developments and events, look at how life changed and indulge in a little nostalgia.

The Monarchy and Empire

Children born at the turn of the century would have had Queen Victoria as their monarch, a loved and respected matriarch whose reign began in 1837. After more than sixty years on the throne she was very much a part of life in Britain at that time. Her death, in January 1901, was the first defining event of the twentieth century. The country, her family and her empire mourned; her state military funeral was a formal, solemn affair with her coffin drawn by six white horses. Victoria was succeeded by her son, Edward VII, who, after fifty-nine years as heir apparent, threw himself into his new role. He travelled widely, being the first British monarch to visit Russia, made several state visits and established the Order of Merit for science, art and literature in 1902. He reigned for just under nine years, however, and died at Buckingham Palace in May 1910. Edward's son became George V, a diligent leader who gained much respect. He visited India in 1911, the first monarch to do so, and was a stable presence during the First World War. In 1917, amidst strong national anti-German sentiment, the royal family abandoned the name Saxe-Coburg-Gotha and adopted the surname Windsor. When King George died in 1935, a year after his Silver Jubilee celebrations, his son Edward, Prince of Wales, was already in a relationship with Wallis Simpson, a married American woman awaiting a divorce. Although Edward wished to marry her, and she was granted a divorce, it was not permissible for the monarch, who was automatically head of the Church of England, to be married to a divorcee. When no state solution could be found, Edward VIII, who had been king for less than a year and was never crowned, abdicated so that he could marry 'the woman I love'. Upon Edward's abdication, his younger brother, George VI, became king. Shy and uncertain, he was thrust into the role but with the support of his young wife Elizabeth, he gradually became more confident and reigned until his death in 1952. As the royal couple had no sons, their eldest daughter became Queen Elizabeth II – our current reigning monarch.

The idea of a day to celebrate the British Empire, which at its height spanned almost a quarter of the populated globe, was first conceived towards the end of Queen Victoria's reign, around 1897. The idea was to remind children 'what it meant to be sons and daughters of such a glorious Empire'. The first Empire Day was declared as 24 May 1902, Queen Victoria's birthday, and in 1916 it became an official annual event marked in schools around the Empire. Children would typically listen to stories of heroism from around the empire, sing patriotic songs, salute the Union

Jack, and partake in ceremonies, concerts, dances and street parties. The Empire Movement, formed by Lord Meath, promoted 'systematic training of children in all virtues which conduce to the creation of good citizens', those virtues being 'Responsibility, Sympathy, Duty and Self-sacrifice'. Until the mid-1950s Empire Day was celebrated annually by millions and was a key day in the national and international calendar. After the decline of the empire the global political landscape changed; with key countries like India gaining independence, Empire Day became gradually less recognised. In 1958 it was renamed British Commonwealth Day and in 1966 it became simply Commonwealth Day, at which time the date was changed to 10 June, the queen's official birthday. Commonwealth Day is now officially the second Monday in March, when the queen broadcasts a message to children of all the Commonwealth countries, but it is far less widely recognised and celebrated than was Empire Day just a few decades ago.

Work, Economy and Welfare

In 1900 the population of Britain was just over 35 million. The economy was stable and unemployment low but still around 25 per cent of people lived in poverty. After the First World War the economy was struggling and there was widespread unemployment, reaching a high of almost 23 per cent in 1933. Although national unemployment improved to around 10 per cent by the end of the 1930s, and industry picked up somewhat in London, the southern counties and the Midlands, widespread economic depression persisted in many areas, particularly Wales, Scotland and the northern counties, until the Second World War, after which the economy gradually improved and industry thrived well into the 1960s. Unemployment fell to a low of around 3 per cent in 1973. During the late 1970s, however, inflation and unemployment rose sharply and recessions persisted during the 1980s and 1990s, with only minimal and short-lived recoveries, although the situation did improve in the last few years of the century.

Privatisation of national industries such as mining, power services and railways affected jobs and the economy in different ways. Traditional industries such as manufacturing declined, while service industries such as hospitality, retail and recreation grew, creating more jobs.

Of the 25 per cent of the population categorised as living in poverty in the early years of the 1900s, around 10 per cent were classed as 'below subsistence level', meaning that they could not afford to eat, buy clothes or pay for rent and fuel. Causes of poverty at this time included sickness, unemployment, extremely low wages, large families and the loss of a main breadwinner. The workhouse was a last resort but was still the only alternative to starvation for many.

Welfare reforms came slowly in a series of changes from around 1906 until 1914: school children were given one free meal per day; small pensions were paid to those aged over 70; sickness benefit was introduced; wages councils were established to set minimum levels of pay for some industries; and unemployment benefit was paid to workers, although only in some trades. After the war the reforms gradually continued, with unemployment benefit being introduced for most workers, except those working in agriculture, who did not receive it until 1936, when levels of this type of work were already in decline. By the end of the 1930s surveys indicated that absolute poverty had declined to less than 4 per cent, partly due to the fact that the cost of living had fallen substantially, and by the century mid-point it was deemed to have all but disappeared. However, the gap between incomes of the rich and the poor widened in the second half of the century. This, together with widespread unemployment, reductions in benefits, recessions and rising costs, meant that poverty was returning.

Life in the Home

At the beginning of the 1900s life at home was very different from that experienced by average families at the end of the century. Many of the labour-saving devices that we take for granted today either did not exist or were much too expensive for the majority of households. Housework that today takes minutes could take hours, even days. Vacuum cleaners, washing machines, fridges, central heating and electricity were not available to most of the population. Most people who were in work and could afford it paid someone to do their washing (taking in washing was a way for many poor women to earn a little extra money) or had at least one young servant to do their housework and help with cooking. A 'spring clean' was common for most households well into the 1960s; this included carpet beating, window cleaning, floor scrubbing and curtain washing.

Many working class people in the early part of the century lived in 'two up, two down' terraced houses with no bathroom and an outside toilet. The downstairs rooms generally consisted of a family kitchen (heated by the coal stove that was used for cooking), where the family gathered and ate, and the 'front room', which was usually out of bounds for children and was used mostly for special occasions or when guests visited. When gas cookers replaced the coal-fired ones, the family focus shifted to the front room, which gradually became the living room, where an open fire was used for heating and also helped to dry clothes in the colder months. Gas lighting was common well into the 1930s and some homes did not have electricity, even for lighting, until the 1950s. By around the mid-1960s, however, more than three-quarters of households had a vacuum cleaner, washing machine and refrigerator and almost all had electricity.

Local authorities started building homes to rent before the First World War and resumed the drive for social housing from the 1920s, with council houses becoming more common after the Second World War, until the Conservative government introduced a policy in 1979 allowing tenants to buy the homes they were renting.

Owning a property was the privilege of around just 10 per cent of the population in 1900, but with rising wages and economic stability, home ownership gradually became popular. Just after the Second World War around 33 per cent of properties were owned and this rose to around 50 per cent in 1970, reaching a peak of almost 70 per cent by the end of the century.

Education
Basic education for all children was widespread in the first decade or so of the twentieth century, although it was common for them to leave school when they were 12 years old; the school leaving age was raised to 14 after the First World War, and to 15 in 1972. The Education Act of 1944 decreed that all children should sit the 11-plus exam, with those who passed going to grammar schools and the others to secondary modern schools. Sitting the 11-plus exam was often a challenging and stressful event for children, with expectations of parents and families sometimes adding to the pressure. Although it was never officially abolished across the UK, the introduction of comprehensive schools in the late 1960s meant that the 11-plus was gradually phased out in many counties.

Corporal punishment was often used on even young children well into the second half of the century. The cane was phased out in primary schools during the 1970s but continued to be used in secondary schools until it was abolished in 1987, although private schools did not completely discontinue its use until 1998.

From the 1950s onwards O levels ('Ordinary') and A levels ('Advanced') were the main qualifications for school and sixth form students respectively. In 1988 O levels – linear exams that were considered difficult for some children, biased towards boys and of only minimal relevance to everyday life – were replaced by GCSEs (General Certificate of Secondary Education), although A levels remained. More exam boards started introducing vocational qualifications that would help young people to gain work. Apprenticeships as a way of training young people in a trade or profession dated back to the Middle Ages, but they regained popularity in the twentieth century; Modern Apprenticeships were launched in 1994 to address UK skills shortages.

University education, which was once only for the elite, started to become a possibility for the middle classes after the First World War, although the number of degrees (fewer than 20,000 per year from 1922 to 1938) did not start to rise until after the Second World War, when the government offered support into higher education for those who had served in the armed forces. With the foundation of many new universities and the introduction of grants, the number of degrees issued steadily rose and by 1991 around 90,000 were awarded. With the restructuring of the higher education system in 1992, which allowed former polytechnics to apply for university status and issue degrees, the number of students completing per year had risen to around 250,000 by the end of the century. Although student grants were discontinued in 1998 and replaced by a loan scheme, university has continued to remain popular. The Open University, founded in 1969, has allowed mature students and those already in work to study part-time for degrees. The first student intake in 1970 was fewer than 50,000, but yearly enrolments doubled by 1988 and the number of qualifications awarded by the OU gradually increased. By the year 2000 around 200,000 students per year were enrolling and to date more than 1.5 million students have been awarded OU qualifications.

Communication and Transport

Telephones were rare in most households until the 1950s but were commonly used in business and public authorities for a couple of decades before this. By 1980 around 70 per cent of UK residents had a landline telephone. Early mobile phones were large, cumbersome and impractical for most people to carry around due to their heavy battery packs, which had long charge times. Although the first call in the world from a cell phone was made in the USA in 1973, there were no calls made in Britain using this medium until 1985. By 1998, however, mobile phones were common, with around 50 per cent of people in Britain owning one (that figure rose to 93 per cent by 2013, with the number of handsets in use, at more than 83 million, overtaking the number of people resident). The beginnings of the modern internet started in Britain in the early 1980s with the work of Sir Tim Berners-Lee and the World Wide Web revolutionised communication. Acorn, Amstrad and Sinclair released computers aimed at schools and individuals throughout the 1980s. The first popular Microsoft Windows computer, developed by IBM, went on sale in 1983 and the Apple Macintosh was released in 1984, creating a rivalry that continues to this day. Email and video calls gave way to social networking, instant messaging, blogs, online forums and internet shopping by the end of the century. By the year 2000 more than 40 per cent of households had a home computer.

At the turn of the century in Britain there were just 8,000 cars. A speed limit of 20 miles per hour was introduced in 1903 and not abolished until 1930. The number of cars rose steadily and by 1930 the number of driving licences issued in London alone was more than 260,000. Cars were still expensive, however, and not affordable for the average family for many years; the Austin 7, released in 1922, cost around £150, the equivalent of more than £8000 today. With an average of 45 miles to the gallon and a maximum speed of 65 miles per hour, it sold well until cheaper American Fords arrived in 1927. The opening of the Dagenham Ford factory in 1929 brought jobs to the East End of London but squeezed British car manufacturing. By 1940 only around 10 per cent of families owned a car and it was not until the 1970s that the majority of households had a car of their own.

Public transport in its various forms was the way to get around for most people in the first half of the century. There were still horse-drawn trams in many towns and cities in 1900, although in the first decade local authorities started to introduce electric trams. Trams were soon overtaken by buses as the most popular form of urban transport but some towns had trolley buses, powered by overhead wires. Buses had both drivers and conductors, who collected passenger fares.

British railways, once a thriving nationalised industry with a branch line in almost every town and village in the country, were decimated after the Beeching report of 1963. When the railways were privatised in the mid-1990s, management of the tracks was split from that of the train services and regional railway companies were formed.

International travel at the start of the 1900s was by steam passenger liner, the most famous being the White Star Line's *Titanic*, which sank on its maiden voyage from Britain to the USA in 1912. The gradual change from coal-fired to oil-powered engines in the 1930s made ships faster and more efficient, but ocean travel was already on the decline.

The first air passenger service between Paris and London was introduced in 1919. Although only a minority of the population travelled abroad in the first half of the century, by the 1960s foreign holidays were starting to become popular and affordable. The idea for a Channel Tunnel was first conceived around 1802 but due to technological, political and financial complications the agreement between Britain and France to build the tunnel was not finalised until 1984. Construction finally began from both the British and French shores in 1988 and the respective tunnels met around the midway point in 1990. The Channel Tunnel was officially opened by the queen and the French president in 1994.

Women and Equality

The lives of women changed immeasurably in the twentieth

century and most of these changes were very much for the better.

The average woman in Britain in 1900 had very few rights or opportunities. Most hoped for little more than to marry well and live to raise their children. At the turn of the century only men were permitted to vote but the National Union of Women's Suffrage had been founded in 1897 by Millicent Fawcett, the educated, feminist wife of Liberal MP Henry Fawcett. Millicent believed in peaceful protest and strong, logical argument to win the right to vote. However, progress was slow, with little support from men with influence, which frustrated many women in the movement. In 1903 Emmeline Pankhurst, together with her daughters Christabel and Sylvia, founded the Women's Social and Political Union. What started with the relatively polite interruption of political meetings and parading of banners escalated to much more drastic measures; suffragettes chained themselves to fences and railings, set fire to churches and public buildings, refused to complete census forms and pay taxes, vandalised and firebombed the clubs and residences of MPs who opposed them and shouted abuse from boats on the Thames when Parliament was in session. Many women were sent to prison for their part in these acts of protest but promptly went on hunger strike to cause embarrassment to the authorities. In 1913 Emily Wilding Davison, a leading campaigner, famously became a suffragette martyr when she was killed after throwing herself in front of the king's horse Anmer during the Epsom Derby. When the First World War was declared the suffragettes halted their campaign, instead working to support the country. In 1918 the Representation of the People Act was passed by Parliament, allowing all women over 30 to vote. Absolute equal voting rights for all women over the age of 21 (the same as men) finally came into force in 1928.

At the same time as the campaign for voting rights, some educated women were trying to qualify in professions and occupations that had previously been solely open to men. The first policewoman with the same powers as her male colleagues was appointed in 1916 and progress continued after the war, when the Sex Disqualification Removal Act was passed allowing women to train and practise as lawyers, surveyors, civil servants and veterinarians. While more young women entered the world of work, it remained uncommon for a woman to work once she was married. This started to change after women proved that they could do the same work as men during the Second World War, and during the 1950s and 1960s many married women worked at least part time as the introduction of labour-saving gadgets such as washing machines and vacuum cleaners made the work of the housewife a little easier. Another campaign for equal pay gained momentum and in 1970 the Equal Pay Act was passed by Parliament, while the Sex Discrimination Act of 1975 meant that employers could not discriminate against women in education, employment or training.

In the first six decades of the twentieth century pregnancy for an unmarried woman was almost always considered a disaster. Health risks aside, women who got themselves 'into trouble' (albeit with the assistance of a man) were often considered immoral and were either shunned and condemned by society or compelled by well-meaning charities and religious organisations to give up their babies for adoption. The passing of the Abortion Act in 1967, together with the introduction of more widely available contraception in the 1970s, meant that gradually women had more choices about if and when to have children.

Before 1923 few women were granted divorce. Men could divorce women relatively easily, particularly for adultery, but it was very difficult for a woman to divorce her husband except on serious grounds such as incest, bigamy or extreme cruelty; adultery alone was not considered grounds for divorcing a man and although this was changed in 1923 the adultery still had to be proved by independent evidence. In 1937 additional grounds of desertion, insanity and drunkenness were permitted as reasons for men or women to seek divorce. The Divorce Reform Act of 1969 led to 'no fault' divorces by mutual consent if a couple had been separated for more than two years.

Overall, by the end of the twentieth century life in Britain had improved for most people. The standard of living of average families had risen significantly, despite three major recessions and two world wars. The founding of the National Health Service in 1948, together with the development of medical drugs, the discovery of vaccines, advances in surgery and greater understanding of nutrition, meant that the general health of the population was greatly improved.

Life expectancy rose from an average of just under 50 years in 1900 to almost 78 in 1999, although this meant a rise in diseases associated with ageing such as dementia and heart disease.

A new century dawned with a population that had almost doubled, to just under 60 million, and for the citizens celebrating the new millennium Britain was a country that their great-grandparents could never have imagined.

Chapter 2

CIVIL RECORDS

Life events – births, marriages, civil partnerships and deaths – are managed by the General Register Office for England and Wales (hereafter referred to as the GRO). Although changes are proposed to the way events can be registered and how much information is made available, at present these records are maintained by district register offices in England and Wales and made available to the public through them (with limited restrictions) and from the GRO headquarters in Southport.

Certificates of birth, marriage and death for our relatives can contain valuable information, some of which might be hitherto unknown. It is a legal offence to knowingly supply false information when events are registered; therefore it is less likely (although not impossible) that the information on a certificate will be inaccurate.

It is a good exercise to examine family certificates in your possession in detail and note the information that was recorded. Is there anything that surprises you or that you didn't know?

Civil Registration History

Registration of births, marriages and deaths is mandatory in the UK. A system of civil registration for England and Wales began with the passing of two Acts of Parliament in 1836: the Marriage Act and the Births and Deaths Registration Act. A Registrar General was appointed and England and Wales were divided into registration districts, each with a number of sub-districts, under the control of a superintendent registrar. On 1 July 1837 (not

1 January) the acts previously mentioned came into force and registration of births, deaths and marriages became compulsory from this date. It was also at this time that register office marriages were first permitted, although at first they happened only rarely. Churches and chapels of all denominations could hold marriage ceremonies, but some also required the presence of a registrar to record the event in the official registers.

In 1874 the Births and Deaths Registration Act came into force. In particular this tightened up the registration of births. Although in theory it was compulsory to register births from July 1837, in practice many parents continued only to baptise their children. From 1874 fines were imposed on parents who did not officially register the birth of a child within six weeks, so records of births became more comprehensive from this date. The above act also specified that unmarried mothers could not name a man as the father of her child unless he was also present. It is estimated that around 10 per cent of marriages in the nineteenth century occurred *after* the birth of the first child.

In 1926 two more Acts of Parliament were passed: the Births and Deaths Registration Act introduced a register of stillbirths, and in order to better regulate burials and prevent trade in or irregular disposal of bodies it also introduced a new system of documentation for burial. The Adoption Act introduced registration of legal adoption in England and Wales from 1927.

From April 1995, under the Marriage Act 1994, it has been possible to get married at other licensed venues apart from churches and register offices, such as stately homes, hotels and castles. The Civil Partnership Act 2004 introduced the legal union of same-sex couples but this was largely superseded by the later Marriage (Same Sex Couples) Act 2013.

Recording and Indexing
Births, marriages, civil partnerships and deaths are recorded in the registration district or sub-district where the event took place.

Although usually this is also where the people lived, this is not necessarily the case; it is the district in which the birth, marriage or death took place. Registers for each life event are completed at the local register office and original copies are kept there.

Copies of the registers of births, marriages, civil partnerships and deaths that have taken place in local districts are periodically sent to the GRO, where they are indexed. These indexes, when complete, are made available to the public at a number of sites.

Until the end of 1983 these alphabetical indexes for each event were compiled quarterly and were available only by searching the volume for each quarter. These quarters are usually referred to by the month in which the quarter finishes, i.e. March, June, September and December for quarters 1, 2, 3 and 4. From 1984 there are annual indexes.

You do not need an index reference to order a certificate if you have details of the event – names, date (even approximate) and places. However, it will be issued more quickly if a reference is provided.

Accessing the Indexes

Complete copies of indexes can be searched at a number of libraries and archives including:

- Manchester City Library:
  www.manchester.gov.uk/info/448/archives_and_local_studies
- Birmingham Central Library:
  www.birmingham.gov.uk/centrallibrary
- Bridgend Local and Family History Centre:
  www1.bridgend.gov.uk/services/libraries/local-and-family-history.aspx
- Plymouth Central Library: www.plymouth.gov.uk/libraries
- City of Westminster Archives Centre:
  www.westminster.gov.uk/services/libraries/archives
- Newcastle City Library: www.newcastle.gov.uk/leisure-

libraries-and-tourism/libraries/branch-libraries-and-opening-hours/city-library
• The British Library, London: www.bl.uk

Visitors to the British Library will need to register for membership, which requires two forms of identification showing a current address.

Indexes up to around 2006 can also be searched online. Sites offering access to indexes (dates vary) include the following. Note that some sites require registration and will charge to view results:

• www.ancestry.co.uk
• www.findmypast.co.uk
• www.freebmd.org.uk
• www.bmdindex.co.uk
• www.familyrelatives.com
• www.thegenealogist.co.uk
• www.ukbmd.org.uk

Interpreting the Indexes
When you have selected the event and the dates that you wish to search, the resulting pages of entries can seem a little confusing with all the columns, abbreviations and codes.

To start searching the indexes you will need to have at least a surname and first name and an idea of the date of the event you are trying to identify. A rough geographical area will also help you find the right entry. As an example, take the births index page from 1960 shown opposite. The surname appears on the index only once, with all registrations for that surname listed underneath in alphabetical order of first name. Where there are two or more registrations for children with the same first name, the middle initial (or initials) determines which is listed first. In this example there are three people called Simon Hall, with the middle initials B, J and R in that order.

HAL		BIRTHS REGISTERED IN JULY, AUGUST AND SEPTEMBER, 1960.								8C
	Mother's Maiden Surname.	District.	Vol.	Page.		Mother's Maiden Surname.	District.	Vol.	Page.	
HALL, Pauline A.	ROSCOW	Stockport	10 a	746	HALL, Sheree S.	FLAVELL	Northampton	3 b	905	
— Pauline A.	HARVEY	Rowley R.	9 b	531	— Shirley	CULLEN	Tynemouth	1 b	796	
— Penelope	O'CONNOR	Nelson	10 e	808	— Shirley A.	HOPE	York	2 d	916	
— Penelope C.	BOWICK	Surrey S.E.	5 g	1201	— Shirley A.	BUCKLESS	Stafford	9 b	632	
— Penelope J.	LINDSAY-SMITH	Kingswood	7 b	777	— Simon B.	TAYLOR	Holderness	2 a	145	
— Penny E.	PAINTER	Derby	3 a	521	— Simon J.	GRAY	Chelmsford	4 a	857	
— Perry R.	CLEMENTS	Northampton	3 b	856	— Simon R.	BASHFORD	Surrey N.E.	5 g	722	
— Peter	MINOR	Birmingham	9 c	636	— Stephen	BEDDELL	Durham E.	1 a	569	
— Peter	MONK	Chesterfield	3 a	235	— Stephen	EADINGTON	Sunderland	1 a	1545	
— Peter B.	AMOS	Swindon	7 c	719	— Stephen	MURPHY	Middlesbro'	1 b	1108	
— Peter D.	GRAINGE	Banbury	6 b	1322	— Stephen	JACKSON	Goole	2 b	829	
— Peter J.	STOREY	Middlesbro'	1 b	1217	— Stephen	GOOCH	Marlboro'	7 c	555	
— Peter J.	FELLOWS	E.Glamorgan	8 b	512	— Stephen	JOYCE	Gateshead	1 a	1184	
— Peter N.	GRIFFITHS	W.Hartlepool	1 a	1632	— Stephen A.	BOWMAN	Durham N.	1 a	640	
— Peter N.	McNIESH	Birmingham	9 c	1035	— Stephen A.	MOORE	Durham C.	1 a	395	
— Peter S.	MUNT	Essex S.W.	5 a	210	— Stephen A.	STAINTON	Lancaster	10 c	674	
— Peter W.	DELANEY	Barkston Ash	2 d	626	— Stephen D.	HALL	Nottingham	3 c	524	0453
— Peter W.	SMALLWOOD	Stoke	9 b	790	— Stephen D.	BURKE	Shrewsbury	9 a	226	
— Philip	WHITE	Sheffield	2 d	352	— Stephen D.	TURNER	Scarboro'	1 b	1311	
— Philip	HALL	Leeds	2 c	378	— Stephen E.	PRETTYMAN	Northallerton	1 b	1237	
— Philip G.	PARDOE	Rowley R.	9 b	462	— Stephen G.	MOONEY	Deptford	5 c	442	
— Philip C.R.	PETER	Wandsworth	5 d	940	— Stephen J.C.	WHITE	Stoke	9 b	860	

Extract from the General Register Office index of births, 1960. (© *Crown Copyright*)

The mother's maiden name is shown in the next column, then the registration district, followed by the district code and the page number. Marriage and death indexes follow a similar format. Below is a list of the information that appears on each type of index, together with examples of entries.

Index of births
Birth indexes are arranged alphabetically by surname. The columns show the following information:

• surname
• first name
• middle initial(s)
• mother's maiden name (from June 1911)
• district where the child was born
• district, code and page number

Here is a transcription of a birth index entry from 1904:

Name	Alfred William White
Registration Year	1904
Registration Quarter	Jan–Feb–Mar
Registration District	Southwark
Volume	1d
Page	27

Index of marriages
Marriage indexes should contain corresponding entries for both partners. The columns show:

- surname
- first name
- middle initial(s)
- surname of spouse
- district where the marriage took place
- district code and page number

Here is a transcription of a marriage index entry from 1942:

Name	Alfred W. Delmar
Spouse Surname	Nicholls
Date of Registration	Apr–May–Jun 1942
Registration District	Stamford
Volume	7a
Page	1255

Index of deaths
Death indexes can help to establish not only whether someone has died but also if they were the right age to be the relative you are looking for. Information is given as follows:

- surname
- first name
- first middle name
- any second middle initial
- age at death (later indexes show actual date of birth)
- district in which the death took place (please note that this is not necessarily where the deceased lived: deaths have to be registered in the district where the person died)
- registration district code and page number

Here is a transcription of a death index entry from 1983:

Name	Alfred Wallis Delmar
Birth Date	20 Dec 1903
Date of Registration	Dec 1983
Age at Death	80
Registration District	St Austell
Volume	21
Page	043

Other indexes

Adoptions – Indexes of adopted children are arranged alphabetically by adopted surname in annual volumes. No indication is given of the date of birth, district of birth or original name. Adoption indexes are not available online but can be viewed and searched at the main repositories mentioned above. Applications for adoption certificates must be made directly to the GRO and orders are subject to restrictions. You can read more about adoption records in my book *Researching Adoption* (Family History Partnership, 2015).

Foundlings – A foundling is a child who was abandoned and whose parentage is not known. There is an Abandoned Children Register for foundlings born since 1977 but no public index is available. Before this, births of abandoned children were registered in the district where the child was found. To obtain a certificate from the Abandoned Children Register you will need to apply in writing to the GRO. There is also a large register (the Thomas Coram Register) of children who were in the care of the Foundling Hospital, London, between 1853 and 1948. Applications for birth certificates of these children can be made to the charity Coram – visit www.coram.org.uk/adoption/your-birth-records or email adoption@coram.org.uk.

Stillbirths – There are no public indexes of stillborn children. Applications for a certificate for a stillborn child will only be issued to a parent or sibling. Contact the GRO directly for details.

Overseas and Armed Forces – Births, marriages and deaths that took place in other countries and were registered by the British Forces, British Consuls or High Commissions are indexed by the GRO but registration of these events is not compulsory outside the country where they took place and therefore the indexes are not comprehensive.

Remember that most of the indexes, especially older ones, are transcriptions from original registers and these have been transcribed again for online searching. Errors and omissions do occur. If you can't locate an entry, always check another source. On Ancestry there is also a browse option so that you can look at digital images of the original indexes. Also, it can help to remember that information in indexes and on certificates may not always be accurate. Living in an age of technology it is difficult (but not impossible) to register events with false information. Before computers and the internet, however, it was easier to provide information to authorities that was not true, as we shall see.

Ordering Certificates

Once you have found a likely index entry for the event you are interested in, you can place an application for the certificate from the GRO (you can also apply without an index entry if you have a good idea of the date and place the event took place). The cost of a full certificate is currently from £9.25, depending on how it is ordered and how much information you have about the event.

Certificates ordered through the GRO standard service can take from three or four working days up to around two weeks, depending on demand and staffing levels. If you require a certificate quickly you can request a priority order, which is despatched the next day if ordered before 4pm. The cost for this priority service is currently £23.40. Certificates can be ordered from the GRO online, by phone or by post; they can also be ordered from the local register office in the district where the event took place – you won't need the reference number if you do this as district register offices do not use the volume and page numbers on the GRO indexes. Information about ordering from the GRO can be found here:

www.gro.gov.uk/gro/content/certificates/contact_us.asp.

To locate the contact details of any register office in England and Wales you can either enter the search term 'Register Office' followed by the place name or use this register office finder website from Direct.Gov:

http://maps.direct.gov.uk/LDGRedirect/MapAction.do?ref=grolight.

Another good site for information about registration districts is:

www.ukbmd.org.uk/genuki/reg/.

Births
Birth certificates give information not just about the child but also about the parents. There are restrictions on ordering certificates for births registered less than fifty years ago, due to GRO anti-fraud measures. If you want to order a birth certificate other than

your own and do not know the exact date and place of birth of the person, you may be questioned about your reason for applying.

REGISTRATION DISTRICT					Southwark				
1904 BIRTH in the Sub-district of Kent Road					in the County of London				
Columns:-	1	2	3	4	5	6	7	8	9	10
No.	When and where born	Name, if any	Sex	Name and surname of father	Name, surname and maiden surname of mother	Occupation of father	Signature, description and residence of informant	When registered	Signature of registrar	Name entered after registration
444	Twentieth December 1903 21 Crosby Row	Alfred William	Boy	Alfred Thomas White	Mary ann White formerly Purdy	House Painter	M. a. White Mother 21 Crosby Row Long Lane Southwark	First February 1904	LM Mather Registrar	

Birth certificate (detail) for Alfred William White, 1903. (© *Crown Copyright*)

Here is a certificate for the birth that relates to the earlier index entry. This is a typical birth certificate from this time. Alfred was born at home, as the majority of children were at that time. His mother was Mary Ann White née Purdy and his father was Alfred Thomas White, a house painter.

Alfred was born on 20 December 1903, but his birth was not registered until 1 February 1904, meaning that this event does not appear in the index until the quarter after it took place. This is not uncommon because six weeks are allowed in which to register a birth, so index entries often appear in the following quarter.

In 1969 the format of birth certificates changed from the traditional 'landscape' shape to the more modern 'portrait' format, with more sections showing additional information. The date and place of birth of the child is given, as well as the name and occupation of the father (modern certificates also give the occupation of the mother), the mother's maiden name, the name and address of the person who registered the birth (usually one or both parents) and the date of registration. New format certificates will also show the place of birth of each parent.

Marriages
A marriage certificate will give the full names and ages of both persons, their occupations, usual addresses and the names and occupations of their fathers. Despite an ongoing campaign, and in an age of supposed equality, still no details about mothers are recorded. The names of at least two witnesses are also recorded. Here is a certificate for a marriage that took place in 1942, which relates to the earlier index entry:

No.	When Married.	Name and Surname.	Age.	Condition.	Rank or Profession.	Residence at the time of Marriage.	Father's Name and Surname.	Rank or Profession of Father.
93	Thirtieth May 19 42	Alfred Wallace Delmar	38 years	Bachelor	No. 5500030 Sergeant Reede Corp (Clerk in Garage)	Wymondham	Alfred Thomas Delmar Deceased	Painter and Decorator
		Dora Elizabeth Nicholls	39 years	Spinster	Manageress of Cafe	41. St. Marys Street Stamford	John Joseph Nicholls	Ironmonger

Married in the Register Office .... by Licence before by me,

This Marriage was solemnized between us, { Alfred W. Delmar / Dora E. Nicholls } In the Presence of us, { Winifred E. Baker / M. Rhymer }   O. M. Allen Registrar. Walter Dellar Supt: Registrar

Marriage certificate (detail) of Alfred Wallace Delmar, 1942. (© *Crown Copyright*)

Alfred Wallace Delmar married Dora Elizabeth Nicholls at the register office in Stanford, Lincoln, on 30 May 1942. He was 38, a bachelor, a sergeant in the army and lived in Wymondham, a town in Norfolk. His father was recorded as Alfred Thomas Delmar (deceased), a painter and decorator.

The similarities between the man on this marriage certificate and the birth of Alfred William White are not a coincidence. The child born in 1903, for reasons unknown, changed his identity to Alfred Wallace (or Wallis) Delmar, sometime between 1911 and 1938 when he enlisted. His children and grandchildren had no idea about his true identity, although he was always evasive about his origins.

Deaths

Modern death certificates give more information than did older versions. The full name and address of the deceased are recorded, together with the place and the cause of death. Since April 1969 certificates have also recorded the date and place of birth of the deceased, plus the maiden name of married women, which makes it easier to connect births with deaths. The name of the informant (the person who registered the death), their address and their relationship to the deceased are also recorded.

Here, to tie up (as far as we are able) the story of Alfred White/Alfred Delmar, is his death certificate:

DEATH		Entry No. 120
Registration district ST. AUSTELL **Sub-district** ST. AUSTELL		Administrative area
		COUNTY OF CORNWALL
1. Date and place of death Twentieth October 1983 North Hill Nursing Home, North Hill Park, St.Austell		
2. Name and surname Alfred Wallis DELMAR	**3. Sex** Male	
	4. Maiden surname of woman who has married -------	
5. Date and place of birth 20thDecember 1903 -----------------------		
6. Occupation and usual address Shop Proprietor(Retired) North Hill Nursing Home, North Hill Park, St.Austell		
7. (a) Name and surname of informant Dora Elizabeth DELMAR	**(b) Qualification** Widow of deceased	

Death certificate (detail) of Alfred Wallis Delmar, 1983. (© *Crown Copyright*)

Note that his date of birth is the same as that given for Alfred William White but even his wife, who registered his death, did not know where he was born.

Author's note: Anyone with information about, or a connection with, the White or Delmar families featured here, please contact the author.

Records in Other Parts of the British Isles

The records described above cover events in England and Wales. Other parts of the British Isles have their own records, each with its own system of indexing, certificate ordering and policy on access to information from the registers.

Scotland

The General Register Office for Scotland is based in Edinburgh. Its website is at www.gro-scotland.gov.uk.

The address for copy certificates of birth, marriage and death is:
New Register House
3 West Register Street
Edinburgh
Scotland
EH1 3YT
Tel. 0131 334 0380

For family and historical research you can visit General Register House at:
2 Princes Street
Edinburgh
Scotland
EH1 3YY
Tel. 0131 535 1314

While civil registration records for Scotland are in some ways superior to those for England and Wales, the indexes give less information and full records must be ordered. Visit www.scotlandspeople.gov.uk to see all the records that are available, including birth, marriage and death indexes, baptisms, burials and wills.

Northern Ireland
The General Register Office for Northern Ireland is located in Belfast. Its website is at www.nidirect.gov.uk/gro and certificates can be ordered online.

The postal address is:
Oxford House
49/55 Chichester Street
Belfast
BT1 4HL
Tel. 028 90 252000

Republic of Ireland
The General Register Office for the Republic of Ireland is located in Roscommon. Its website is at www.welfare.ie/en/Pages/General-Register-Office.aspx.

The address is:
Government Offices
Convent Road
Roscommon
Ireland
Tel. (from the UK) 353 90 6632900

Divorce

Details contained in modern divorce records are never made available to the public. A decision was taken in the late 1930s that documents relating to divorce were far too private ever to be read by anyone else. Therefore very few divorce papers after 1937 are available for public consultation. A high percentage of historical divorce records for England from 1858 to 1937 do survive. Indexes are available online and microfilms of original documents can be viewed at the National Archives in Kew, London – see www.nationalarchives.gov.uk/records/looking-for-person/ divorce.htm for more information.

From 1938 there are limited records available about divorces.

Only confirmation that a couple have divorced, in the form of a copy of the decree absolute, can be obtained. To order a copy of a decree absolute you will need to provide not just the names of both parties but also the date and place of their marriage, so unless you know these details exactly it will be necessary first of all to order a copy of the couple's marriage certificate. The current cost for a ten-year search, including a copy of the decree absolute if found, is £65, which seems very expensive when compared with certificates and wills, especially when the information gained is limited.

The decree absolute will not contain details of addresses at the time of the divorce; it simply shows that two people who married on a certain date are now divorced. If another person was involved in the divorce as a third party (where adultery was the reason for the divorce), they might be named as the co-respondent. This often provides a clue to a subsequent marriage. Remember also that these days it is common for women to revert to their maiden name once they are divorced. For more information about divorce records read this research guide from the National Archives: http://www.nationalarchives.gov.uk/records/looking-for-person/divorce.htm.

How to obtain copies of modern divorce decrees
Copies of decrees absolute can be ordered by post from the Central Family Court (previously known as the Principal Registry of the Family Division). Full instructions can be found here: www.gov.uk/copy-decree-absolute-final-order.

Divorce records in Scotland
Records of divorce up to 1984 are held at the National Records of Scotland (previously the National Archives of Scotland). Their website is at www.nrscotland.gov.uk.

Complications

There are always complications, pitfalls and potential brick walls when undertaking family research, but perhaps particularly so when searching for records relating to recent ancestors and living relatives. For example, the social norms regarding names at the beginning of the twentieth century, whereby a woman took her husband's surname upon marriage and a child took its parents' surname at birth, no longer necessarily applied by the end of the century. Women often now keep their maiden name when they marry, or couples combine their surnames into one, hyphenated name. Additionally, sometimes people will adopt completely unrelated surnames, just because they like them and don't particularly like the one they were born with or inherited through marriage. First names can also be a minefield, but this has been the case for centuries. Pet names, nicknames, middle names used as first names and changing forenames to suit is as common now as ever. I have two examples in my own family where the name that a relative was known by wasn't their real one.

It isn't a modern idea that 'you can become who you want to be', as the example of Alfred Delmar shows; in today's world, however, where personal choice often comes above obligation to conform, most things are possible.

Jacob's Story

Jacob was originally called Mark, a name his mother liked and chose for him when he was born in the early 1970s. Mark, however, did not feel the same about it. He says, 'I never liked my name – I thought it was boring and it didn't suit me at all.' A couple of decades ago, when he was in his late 20s, Mark read a book in which the main character was called Jacob. He loved the book, identified with this character and later, when he thought about changing his name, Jacob was the obvious choice. He says 'changing my name wasn't exactly an act of rebellion, but I was changing and growing in lots of ways. I had

28

little in common with my parents and this was a stand for independence.' The practical side was easy enough: a visit to a solicitor, a declaration and a few letters to official bodies. Getting used to the name came naturally too: 'I felt like Jacob from day one,' he says, 'and never looked back'. His friends and relatives took a little longer to get used to it and his parents took a while to accept it, but eventually everyone came round and now 'Mark' belongs firmly in the past.

Changes to Come
The General Register Office was established in 1837, the first year of Queen Victoria's reign. Although there have been many changes to the registration system over the years concerning the recording of information, the format of certificates and the procedure for issuing them, keeping pace with life in modern Britain remains a challenge for civil registration. Each new change in the law requires the introduction of new procedures.

Legislation on civil partnerships and same-sex marriage has been introduced in recent years. A campaign fought in 2014 resulted in a promise by the prime minister to address the fact that details only of the fathers of brides and grooms were recorded on marriage certificates. Plans are now under way to change the format of marriage certificates so that the mothers' names are also recorded. Ongoing scientific breakthroughs in fertility treatment and genetics, such as egg or sperm donation and DNA replacement resulting in three-parent children, may also result in legislation to allow additional information on birth certificates.

An ambitious project was started in 2005 to scan and produce digital images of birth, marriage and death records so that they could be ordered and viewed online. The contract, lasting three years, managed to complete digitisation of only around half of the records and work was halted. Further initiatives followed, which planned to complete and improve on the first project, but in 2012, due to rising costs and cuts in funding, the work was halted indefinitely.

Parish Registers

Before civil registration records began in 1837, there were church records of baptisms, marriages and burials. When civil registration was introduced, however, the recording of life events in parish registers did not cease – in fact, churches and other independent places of worship continue to keep these records today.

A number of indexes, transcriptions of register entries and even some digital images of original registers for the twentieth century are available online, particularly for the early part of the century.

Parish register transcriptions (and sometimes digital images) can be found on Find My Past, Ancestry, Family Search (www.familysearch.org) and other private and volunteer-run sites, although very few of these go beyond around 1920. Here is an example, downloaded from Ancestry, of a marriage register from the London parish of St Augustine for 1921:

Marriage register entry, James Hoyle to Hannah Fitzsimmons, 1921. (© *Liverpool Record Office*; *reproduced by courtesy of Ancestry.com*)

What is particularly nice about this image is that it contains not just information about the event and the people involved, but also features the original signatures of the bride, groom and the witnesses.

The Church of Jesus Christ of the Latter-day Saints (also known as the Mormons) has records relating to millions of family history documents from all over the world. Many of these are parish records of baptisms, marriages and burials. Consider this typical entry for a baptism that took place in 1911:

Name:	Ruth Lilian Watkins
Gender:	Male
Christening Date:	20 Sep 1911
Christening Place:	St John's Church, Fishponds, Gloucester, England
Birth Date:	31 Aug 1903
Father's Name:	Ambrose Isaac Watkins
Mother's Name:	Ellen

Note that, as is often (but not always) the case, the child's date of birth, in addition to the baptism date, is included. Also, the gender of 'Ruth' is recorded as male, which is almost certainly incorrect! The information contained in this free entry could lead a relative to other records about the family.

The project to collect names and data for Family Search is ongoing and inclusive; anyone who has carried out their own family research is welcome to add their own details and those of their living and recently deceased family members. The website www.familysearch.org helped me to find living relatives in Canada when all I had was the name and date of death of a great aunt. The International Genealogical Index (IGI) forms a major part of this site and incorporates the British Isles Vital Records Index – for a good description of these collections and what they contain visit www.familysearch.org/learn/wiki/en/Great_Britain_ Vital_Records_Index_(FamilySearch_Historical_Records).

However, note that information from Family Search will usually be index entries, transcriptions or member-submitted content. Therefore, without further evidence (such as copies of original register entries), information from this site, particularly entries submitted by members, should not alone be considered proof of family connections.

It is sometimes possible to view original or copy registers in the actual places where family events took place, especially parish churches. This can be helpful if you want to browse and take photographs of registers or make notes from them. Permission to access these records, however, varies widely. Arrangements need to be made with those in charge of the records and some places may ask for a fee or donation for their time and trouble. I have a good example of this from a previous case.

A Changing Surname

Tony Mariner was born in the early 1930s and his nephew, Matthew Mariner, acted as executor to his estate when he died a few years ago. Matthew knew that his paternal family had some Italian heritage, but his father Gerald (Tony's younger brother) had died when Matthew was a teenager and he knew little more than that. He came to me because he was unable to find his uncle's birth certificate. Although Matthew was quite sure that Tony was born in Southampton, neither the GRO nor the local register office could trace a record of his birth. The marriage certificates of Tony and Gerald confirmed that they were Catholics and that they were married in the same church within a few years of each other. The administrator at the church was very helpful and allowed me to visit to take a look at the registers of baptisms, marriages and burials. The entry for Tony's marriage recorded several witnesses, including one Giuseppe Mariano. This led me to the discovery of a large number of parish records relating to an extended family called Mariano, which included the baptism of Antonio Mariano ('Tony Mariner'). I was able to document, through these records, how the family members changed their surname from

Mariano to Mariner over the course of a year in the late 1930s, in the time leading up to the Second World War. The parish registers not only helped to solve the puzzle of the 'missing' birth certificate, they also gave Matthew some insight into his Italian heritage.

Chapter 3

THE CENSUS

Census records have long been one of the most popular resources for tracing ancestry, and rightly so. The information about households and families that was recorded on census returns is as invaluable as it is unique; so far, with every census that has been released, more details have emerged about the people who were living in Britain a century or more ago.

A History of the Census
In its most basic form, a census is an official count or survey of a population. It can be as simple as a headcount, but usually there is information contained therein that can be invaluable to family research. Censuses in some form or another have been taken worldwide for thousands of years; in the Bible Mary and Joseph were travelling to their home town to be counted in a census when Jesus was born. The information collected in a census was often statistical and used for determining labour force numbers or planning supplies of housing and provisions, for example. The modern census has been taken in the UK every ten years since 1841 (except for 1941) and the recorded information is released to the public after 100 years of closure. These documents provide a snapshot of a day in the life of our ancestors' households in each decade. The format and information recorded changed slightly in each decade but the returns for each household generally show who lived in a property, with whom, how old they were, where they were born and what they did for a living.

One important thing to remember when looking at census

returns is that the information recorded may not necessarily be completely truthful or accurate. Ages may have been adjusted, occupations made to sound more important, relationships invented or ignored, information conveniently forgotten and euphemisms used to present a version of the family that the householder wished to convey. Also, the census recorded people who were present in the household on the night of the date that the census relates to; it was not a record of those who were usually resident. Therefore, family members who were travelling, studying or working away might not appear as resident at their usual address. Sunday was usually chosen as census day as traditionally it was the day of the week when people were most likely to be at home. In the days leading up to the census night, blank forms were distributed to every address in each district by an official called an enumerator, who instructed householders to complete them on the night of the census. After the night of the census, checking and collection of the completed forms would begin, with enumerators ensuring that all sections of the form had been filled in correctly before the information was sent to the office of the Registrar General in London.

There were separate censuses for England, Wales, Scotland, Ireland, the Channel Islands and the Isle of Man, although they were all taken on the same dates and the format of documents was similar.

The census returns for England and Wales from 1841 to 1911 have been indexed, transcribed and digitally photographed and are available to search and view on the internet. Quality and accuracy can vary, however, and while information on some sites is free, access to full details and digital images sometimes incurs a charge. The information on some sites is derived from transcriptions by volunteers who have experience of reading handwriting, deciphering occupations and a knowledge of place names. Some commercial sites offering census data, however, engage people who might not have any experience with (or interest in) historical records to transcribe them, which can result in inaccurate index entries.

The main websites offering UK census information are:

- www.ancestry.co.uk
- www.findmypast.com
- www.thegenealogist.co.uk
- www.freecen.org.uk
- www.familysearch.org
- www.ukcensusonline.com
- www.scotlandspeople.gov.uk
- www.census.nationalarchives.ie

For more information read the guide to census records issued by the National Archives: www.nationalarchives.gov.uk/records/research-guides/census-returns.htm.

The Census of 1901

This census was taken on the night of Sunday, 31 March 1901, and details of more than 32 million people in 6 million households were recorded.

A form called a schedule was left with every householder, to be collected after census night. District enumerators then transcribed all the information from these schedules into enumeration books. Digital images of these books can be accessed online, although the original household schedules for 1901 were destroyed. Information for more than one household appears on each page, with the address of the properties in the second column (the first column being a running schedule number). The details that were recorded for each individual in the household were:

- Name (forename and surname)
- Relationship to the head of family (usually the oldest male)

- Condition as to marriage
- Age last birthday (the column in which age was recorded indicated whether male or female)
- Profession or occupation
- Employer, worker or own account
- If working at home
- Where born (county and parish or country)

In both England and Wales there was an additional column to indicate disabilities. The heading used some terms that would not be considered correct today, such as Deaf and Dumb, Blind, Lunatic, Imbecile and Feeble Minded.

In Wales there was an additional column to record the language spoken (English, Welsh or both). In Scotland and Ireland this column recorded whether Gaelic or Irish respectively was spoken, while in Ireland there was also a separate column for religion.

British ships, hospitals, workhouses, barracks and residential institutions had their own separate enumeration books.

The following is a census entry for a fairly typical London household in 1901 – one that happens to feature the ancestors of one of our most famous citizens. The Beckham family lived at 3 Victory Cottages in Newington. William Beckham, great-great-grandfather of David, was the head of the household; he was 30, worked as a 'Vestry Carman' (driver of a council horse-drawn vehicle) and was born in London, Newington. Also present in the house on census night were his wife Harriet, 27, and his children Martha, Jane, Mary and William.

By 1911 the Beckham family had grown considerably and had moved to 37 Eltham Street, Walworth. (This street, together with those surrounding it, was demolished in 1980 to extend an inner city park called Nursery Row.) For this census, each household was recorded on a separate form. William Beckham, by then aged 41, worked as a 'Carman' for the Boro (sic) Council. His

Census image (detail) showing the Beckham family in Newington, 1901. (© *The National Archives RG13/378/15/21; reproduced by courtesy of Ancestry.com*)

handwriting was perfectly neat and legible, as was his signature. He and his wife Harriet had been married for twenty years and had had ten children, eight of them still living. Six of the surviving children, aged from 5 to 19, also lived at the address. Recorded on the census for the first time was Edward Beckham, aged 8, who was David Beckham's great-grandfather. William Beckham's parents, John and Sarah, were also living in this family home. It is interesting to note that, at the age of 65, John was still working for the council and was employed as a 'Scavenger'.

The following year, three of the boys in this family would be involved in a fatal tragedy. On an outing with the boy scouts, William Beckham, a patrol leader, together with younger brothers Edward and James, was rowing on the Thames when their boat overturned. Edward and James were saved by their scoutmaster, but William drowned, along with seven other boys from Walworth between the ages of 11 and 14. A memorial to these boys (pictured on the front cover) now stands in Nunhead Cemetery in Southwark, London. Edward, aged 11 at the time of the tragedy, eventually joined the navy and became a chief petty officer. His son, Aubrey Edward Jack Beckham, David's grandfather, was born in 1925 and also became a seaman.

Census image showing the Beckham family in Walworth, 1911. (© *The National Archives RG14/1809/RD23/SD4/ED17/SN389; reproduced by courtesy of Ancestry.com*)

Later Censuses

The 1911 census is, at the time of writing, the latest census to be released and available for research purposes. A census has continued to be taken in the UK every ten years since then (with the exception of 1941) but these are held in confidential government archives without, at present, any possibility of early release. The Census Act 1920 introduced a strict 100-year closure without exception on every subsequent census. The Office for National Statistics will not consider requests under Freedom of Information legislation for information about relatives or ancestors from any post-1920 census.

The official release date of the 1921 census will be 1 January 2022. This will cover England, Wales, Scotland, the Channel

Islands and the Isle of Man. The Irish Free State, officially founded in 1919, did not hold a census in 1921; the first Irish census was held in 1926 and is not due for release until January 2027. However, there have been attempts to obtain its release as early as 2016 and a final decision is yet to be made. Northern Ireland also held its own census in 1926 but personal records that were collected at that time no longer exist; they are thought to have been destroyed during the Second World War as part of a government policy to reduce fire risk.

Traditionally, the census was conducted in the spring and the 1921 census was due to take place on 24 April. However, due to a strike by transport workers and miners, census day was postponed for two months, taking place instead on Sunday, 19 June 1921. There was some concern that a summer date would result in more people being recorded away from home and this does seem to have been the case in certain areas, with the population of some seaside towns considerably higher. Statistical information from the census shows an overall population increase of almost 5 per cent from 1911 to almost 43 million. There were some new questions asked in this census: the exact place of work rather than just the type of industry, and for children under 15 their 'orphanhood' status (whether one or both parents had died). Divorce was added as a marital status option, but questions about length of marriage, number of children and infirmity were not included in this census. Find out more about the 1921 census at: www.1921census.org.uk.

There was a census taken in 1931 but returns for England and Wales were destroyed by fire in 1941; only the 1931 census for Scotland survives. No census was taken in 1941 because of the war.

The 1939 Register
The loss of the 1931 census and the absence of a census in 1941 creates a long period for which this valuable information is unavailable. Thankfully for researchers and amateur family

historians, the 1939 Register goes some way to bridging this gap. With war approaching, the National Registration Bill was introduced and passed swiftly through Parliament, coming into force just two days before the war began. The purposes of registration were threefold: to analyse population distribution for manpower control and in anticipation of the need for evacuation, to obtain accurate population figures and to facilitate the introduction of rationing.

Friday, 29 September 1939 was National Registration Day. The information recorded was similar to that on the census, with each person asked to state the following:

• Name
• Address
• Sex
• Date of birth
• Marital status
• Occupation
• If a member of armed forces or reserves

Registration forms were distributed by district enumerators. When these forms were collected, each resident was given a buff-coloured identity card. Around 46 million identity cards were issued. Each card bore a unique card number consisting of the enumeration district code, the running line number from the schedule and the household person number. Some people who, for example, needed access to restricted areas were later issued with replacement green cards containing a photograph and description of the holder. In 1943 replacement blue cards were issued that combined registration with rationing. Although the war ended in 1945, rationing continued for some time. Manpower was not considered high enough to increase food production, and strikes, particularly by dockworkers, were frequent, affecting imports, while poor weather conditions limited the post-war

The form that every householder had to complete in 1939. (© *FindMyPast.co.uk*)

harvest of wheat and potatoes. ID cards were abolished in 1952, when the National Registration Act was repealed, and rationing finally ended in 1954.

Accessing the 1939 Register

In 2014 Find My Past, in partnership with the National Archives, began an ambitious project to scan, digitise and index the 40 million entries in 7,000 original volumes. This long-awaited record set was released in October 2015 and gives access to transcriptions and digital images of the original returns for anyone who is now over 100 years old, or whose death has been confirmed. The index is free to search but the full record for a household is £6.95 to view and download, although discounts are available for multiple purchases. Visit www.findmypast.co.uk/1939register for further information about how to search and to check current charges for viewing and downloading records.

Chapter 4

DIRECTORIES AND REGISTERS

Directories and registers help us to discover where our relatives lived, for how long and what they did, helping us to locate them at specific times and places, and to build a picture of them at home and at work.

What are Directories and Registers?

A simple definition of a directory is 'a book or website listing individuals or organisations alphabetically or thematically with details such as names, addresses, and telephone numbers'.

A register is 'an official list or record of names or items' – synonyms include inventory, record, ledger, archive, catalogue, schedule, roll, roster and listing. One might think of a school register, parish register or electoral register, for example.

Electoral Registers

Also known as voters' lists, these are registers of people who are eligible to vote in households within a parliamentary constituency. They can help to confirm who was resident at an address at a particular time.

Until 1918 only males over the age of 21 who were property owners or wealthy tenants were allowed to vote in general elections. Female property owners or rate payers were only allowed to vote in local elections. As a result of the Representation of the People Act 1918, all resident males over the age of 21 and resident females over the age of 30 were given the vote. In 1928, mainly as a result of the suffrage movement, women were given the same voting rights as men and the age was lowered to 21 for females. This continued to be the case until the voting age for all adults was lowered to 18 in 1970.

To be eligible to vote today a person must be aged 18 or over, a British, Irish or Commonwealth citizen and resident in the UK. British citizens living abroad are also eligible to vote by post or proxy for up to fifteen years after they leave the UK, but registration is voluntary. Their names will appear on the electoral register in the constituency where they were last resident. EU citizens resident here can vote in local, but not general, elections. Visitors from outside the EU and convicted prisoners are not entitled to vote. Members of the House of Lords may vote in local elections, but not in general elections.

The following website has detailed information about voting rights and electoral registers: www.electoralcommission.org.uk.

Historical Registers
Electoral registers usually record the first name, middle initial and surname of people in a given household who were eligible to vote during the period in which the register was current. Some older registers recorded full names, including middle names. Registers were traditionally compiled in the autumn, with a cut-off date in October, and were published in the following February. They were valid for a year. Now that records are compiled and updated electronically, it is possible to update information more regularly.

Information that was recorded about voters, even many years ago, can be extremely useful in helping to trace a person or provide information about a family. For example, if you are researching an ancestor named in family documents as 'Millie Brookes' who lived at a particular address fifty years ago, the historical electoral register might tell you that her first name is Millicent, her middle initial is D and the name of her husband was Timothy Brookes. This confirms not only Millie's name and the spelling but also her husband's. You could then search for their marriage, children and deaths to extend the research in more than one direction.

Sometimes families lived in a house for decades, even generations, and much information can be gained about family members who came of age, left home, married or died by tracking the names that appear in and disappear from the register. Until 1948 business owners with separate premises had an additional vote connected with that address, indicated in the registers by the initials BP.

Historical electoral registers were printed by local authorities and many survive in a bound format. They are in volumes according to parliamentary constituency and arranged alphabetically by street within each ward of the constituency. Therefore, it is necessary to know the address, or at least the road, where a person lived in order to check the entry for their household in the register. The survival and availability of historical registers varies a great deal between different areas of Britain. They are often held in county or city libraries, archives and heritage centres.

The following is a digital image of a section from the Kensington electoral register of 1929 showing entries for writer and poet Siegfried Sassoon and his neighbours. The abbreviations used are: Occupier (O), Resident (R), Wife (W), Wife who qualified through her husband's occupation (Dw) and Special Juror (SJ) .

Some local authorities have an almost complete set of registers for their area dating back to before 1900; others have just a handful of registers from recent decades. Policy on access varies also, as local government officers interpret laws on data protection in different ways. Some authorities have an 'open access' policy and are happy to look up entries for households in response to enquiries by telephone, letter or email. Staff at other authorities may be less willing to give information from registers over the telephone or have a time-scale policy to answer

		HOLLAND WARD.	POLLING DIS
Rw	—	Barnett, Bertha	2C CA
R	O	Bridges, Edward	20
		Ettingdene—**SJ**	
Rw	Dw	Bridges, Katherine Dianthe	20
Rw	—	Foote, Myrtle May	20
Rw	—	Chapman, Mary Elizabeth	21
Rw	—	Edwards, Edith Alice	21
Rw	Dw	Macpherson, Alice Bessie	21
R	O	Macpherson, Arthur Holte	21
Rw	—	Deane, Amy	22
R	D	**Turner, George (Col.)**	22
Rw	Ow	**Turner, Maud**	22
R	O	Whelpdale, Arthur	22
		William	
Rw	Dw	Whelpdale, Beatrice Lilian	22
Rw	—	Butler, Minnie	23
R	—	Butler, William	23
R	—	Sassoon, Siegfried	23
Rw	Dw	Speed, Clara	23
R	O	**Speed, Harold—SJ**	23
Rw	—	Taylor, Maud	23
Rw	—	Gisby, Ada Ann Borton	24
R	O	**Hind, Arthur Mayger—SJ**	24
Rw	Dw	**Hind, Dorothy Alice**	24
Rw	—	Yaxley, Reda May	24

Extract from the 1929 electoral register for Kensington. (© *Royal Borough of Kensington and Chelsea Libraries*)

enquiries. Sometimes library staff will do short searches for free but many authorities now charge for research services, and the costs vary.

Electoral Registers at the British Library
A national collection of UK electoral registers from 1947 is held by the British Library in London. Availability is subject to change

as some older registers have been moved to another site and need to be ordered in advance. See this detailed British Library Guide website for current information: www.bl.uk/reshelp/findhelp restype/offpubs/electreg/electoralregisters.pdf.

Visitors to the British Library will need to apply for a reader pass, which requires two forms of identification with a current address to be produced.

If you are not able to visit the British Library yourself or get someone to search the registers on your behalf, there is a charged look-up service. To find out more about how to order this service, email research@bl.uk or telephone 020 7412 7903.

Online Registers

When electoral registers were first made available to the public on CD and via the internet in the mid-1990s they were a revelation – anyone in the UK could use these discs or databases and researchers were saved from hours of trawling through volumes at local libraries. Unfortunately, researchers were not the only ones using these resources. Companies used them to compile mailing and cold calling lists, people used them to find relatives and lost loves who did not want to be found and the awareness was dawning that this information, collected by local authorities as a statutory requirement, was being sold to absolutely anyone, arousing anger and indignation. Now, under the Representation of the People Act (Regulations 2002), voters have the right to request that their details are not sold or made available in registers for public consultation, rather like having an unlisted phone number. Now there are two copies of each register, one full register, available only to the local authority for voting purposes and to credit reference agencies to prevent fraud, and one edited register. Around 45 per cent of the population who register to vote opt out of the public register and details of their addresses are not made available.

There are a number of services offering online searches for UK residents based on electoral register data. Find My Past has electoral registers from 2002, in the Census, Land and Surveys category, at: http://search.findmypast.co.uk/search-world-Records/uk-electoral-registers-2002-2014.

Find My Past has also recently released a collection called England & Wales, Electoral Registers 1832–1932. These records are from more than 150 million registers held by the British Library and are searchable by name, year, constituency, polling district and county. You will find these electoral registers on www.findmypast.co.uk under Census, Land and Surveys on the Search page.

Ancestry.co.uk has an ongoing initiative to scan electoral registers for the UK and the first of these substantial collections are now available to search and download: London registers up to 1965 (not including former counties that are now part of Greater London), Midland registers up to 1955 (Birmingham and North Warwickshire) and North Yorkshire registers up to 1962. The registers are indexed electronically using text recognition software, so some searches, even using the correct names, can be negative. The advantage is that you can search by road or building name to identify residents.

192 – www.192.com – is an established online service with phone directory, electoral register and company director information. To search for a person on this site is free but you must purchase credits to view the results. You will need to register and buy a minimum number of credits. For premium information, such as historical electoral register data, an extra fee is payable.

Another alternative is People Tracer – www.peopletracer.co.uk. Again, credits are needed for each search.

Street Directories
Directories of businesses in towns and counties were first published in the 1700s but were sporadic, sometimes cheaply produced and often incomplete. The first regular publisher of

trade directories was Pigot's, founded in 1814, which continued trading until 1835. Early directories contained a geographical description of an area, its main trades, inns, churches, landowners, coach routes and postal times. Frederic Kelly was inspector of letter carriers in 1836, which oversaw publication of the Post Office London Directory. He set up Kelly & Co., which produced county directories and expanded over a few decades, taking over various small district, town and city directory publishers until his company had an almost complete monopoly of the directories business.

Changing its name to Kelly's Directories Ltd in 1897, the company went from strength to strength. Directories became larger, including more information not only about trades and

Kelly's Directory
for Portsmouth and
Southsea, 1926–27.

professions but also about residents. Profit was made by the sale of advertising and also through the sale of directories to businesses and individual residents.

An invaluable resource for researchers everywhere, street directories mostly ceased publication in the 1970s when they became unprofitable but they continued to be produced for London until the mid-1980s. They listed local residents alphabetically by name, giving their address, and also had a section arranged by street listing all the businesses and private residents. In this extract from a Hampshire directory at the turn of the century, the residents of this small street in Southampton were a diverse group of tradesmen including a watchmaker, a saddler, a plumber, a hairdresser and a beer retailer. There was also an 'oyster bar' (traditionally a seafood restaurant or cafe that specialises in serving oysters).

The entries were limited to one person per household, usually the 'head' (man) or sometimes the main resident or property owner. Entries from these directories can help to confirm exact addresses or establish how long a family remained resident at a particular property.

Many county and main city libraries and archives have comprehensive runs of old street directories. For details of libraries, visit the website of the local authority where your family lived – for

Extract from a street directory showing residents of a Southampton street, *c.* 1900.

```
..........here is Salem rd.........
Pound Tree lane, 72 Above
     Bar to Sussex road.
         NORTH SIDE.
   Compton Wm. Hy. surgn
 1 Cox John T. M. hair dressr
 2 Lovejoy Charles, beer ret
 3 Lovejoy Charles, oyster bar
 4 Hussey Humphrey, plumbr
 5 Cromar Henry & Co. watch
     makers
 6 Rogers Edward, antique
     furniture dealer
 7 Yearsley Henry, beer retlr
     Berry Wm. Geo. saddler
Prince's road, Freemantle,
     45 Park road.
24 Pearce Captain John
24 Pearce Miss Myra, certifi-
     cated nurse
Princes street, Northam,
   Northam rd. to Millbank st.
         NORTH SIDE.
13 Luckhurst John, shoe ma
...... here is Cobourgs st ......
67 Cook Henry, shopkeeper
   Pellerin Auguste, margar-
     ine manufacturer
```

50

example, entering the search term 'Hampshire Libraries' or 'Hampshire Archives' should bring the top result of the county council website page for that service. Alternatively, council website home pages usually have an A–Z index of services where you can locate library and record office details.

Enquiries by phone or email for one-off searches in a directory are often free but policy does vary between authorities and there may be a delay in the response time.

The Society of Genealogists library in London has an extensive range of street directories covering most areas of England and Wales. Members have free access to collections but visitors can purchase an hourly or day pass to use the library. Take a look at the Society's website for more information about this and other collections in the library: www.sog.org.uk or call 020 7251 8799.

Some street directories have been digitally scanned and images of the pages are available online, although these are mostly older directories. Produced originally with lottery funding by the University of Leicester, www.historicaldirectories.org is one of the more comprehensive sites but only covers parts of England and Wales and features directories up to 1919 only. There is a new URL for this site but the old address should forward to the new site: http://specialcollections.le.ac.uk/cdm/landingpage/collection/p16445coll4.

A few local authorities have also digitised their street directories and made them available online. The Portcities site for Southampton – www.portcities.org.uk – has viewable and searchable street directories up to the 1970s.

Telephone Directories

The demise of the street directory overlapped with the rise in private telephone use. The public telephone service was introduced in 1879 and the first telephone directory was published the following year. It was not until well into the 1950s, however, that household telephones became popular and directories became widely used. From that time, when more ordinary householders subscribed to a telephone service, to the mid-1980s, almost everyone with a telephone was listed in the directory covering the area where they lived. Usually only the titled, the very rich or those with sensitive professions, such as policemen and politicians, had unlisted (ex-directory) numbers. Anyone could have an unlisted phone number but it was not free, so few ordinary people did.

Once companies discovered how to use directories to sell to householders, however, the percentage of ex-directory numbers increased annually in an attempt to stop unsolicited sales calls. From just 5 per cent of unlisted numbers in 1975, the total increased to around 70 per cent in 2000.

Entries in telephone directories give only the surname, initials, address and telephone number of the subscriber – usually the person who paid the bill. Historical directories are often kept in local libraries for the area that they cover but an almost complete set of directories for the whole of the UK from the late 1800s to date is kept at the British Telecom Archives in Holborn Telephone Exchange, London: www.btplc.com/Thegroup/BTsHistory/BT grouparchives. The archive does not offer a research service and access to the collection is in person only. It is best to book an appointment by email in advance via archives@bt.com and photographic ID is required before access is granted.

In partnership with BT, Ancestry.co.uk has digitised images from telephone directories from the British Phone Books Collection, 1880–1984. These are also indexed and searchable by name.

In addition, there are several searchable online sources for current telephone directories; the official version for the UK is provided by BT at: www.thephonebook.bt.com, while Infobel offers links to directories not only in the UK but also worldwide: www.infobel.com/en/world.

Dictionary of National Biography (DNB)

The *Dictionary of National Biography* has been in print and widely used in public libraries for decades. First published in 1885, it has now been renamed the *Oxford Dictionary of National Biography*, runs to sixty volumes in hard copy, and lists almost 60,000 entries for notable figures from British history. It is not only famous or well-known people who have entries in these volumes: musicians, entrepreneurs, sportsmen and women, authors, actors, honoured servicemen and women, researchers, engineers and local heroes are all likely to be included. If your ancestor was recognised for any achievement, received an honour or was in any way well known, it is worth searching this work. There is an online edition, which is searchable by name and location, but this requires a subscription. Most main public libraries have free access, however, and members might be able to access this from home via their library website. To find out more visit: http://global.oup.com/oxforddnb.

Who's Who/Who Was Who

Published annually since 1849, *Who's Who* contains biographical information on around 33,000 prominent people worldwide who are held in esteem or have influenced British life. Notable individuals including academics, politicians, judges, athletes, artists, authors, scientists and actors are included. Once someone has an entry in *Who's Who*, it is never removed, even if they retire or leave their position. When a person with an entry in *Who's Who* dies, their biography is removed and is subsequently included in a volume called *Who Was Who*; the entry is duplicated as it last appeared in *Who's Who* but with the date of death included at the end. *Who Was Who* was produced in one complete volume covering 1897 to 1915, every ten years until 1990 and every five years thereafter. Libraries and institutions can subscribe to Who's Who Online – www.ukwhoswho.com – so their library members and visitors are able to access this site free of charge.

Chapter 5

WILLS

Wills and administrations have long been a favourite resource for family history research. Although only around 40 per cent of people make a valid will, there is a good chance that at least one of your ancestors left one. Using documents relating to the distribution of an estate after death we can discover not just information about our relatives and their assets but also any details recorded about their executors and beneficiaries.

One advantage with this type of record is that, unlike so much potentially useful material about the recent past, they are not covered by Data Protection legislation, which only relates to living people.

Let's have a look at some of the terminology used and what it means:

Administration – The process of collecting assets, paying debts and distributing the deceased's estate.

Beneficiaries – A person (who may or may not be a relative) who receives money or other assets from the deceased in accordance with instructions in the will (this might also be an organisation or charity).

Codicil – A legal document amending or updating a previous will, but not replacing it.

Estate – The property, money and possessions of a person who has died.

Executor – A person appointed in a will to administer the estate of a deceased person.

Grant of Representation - Permission from the Probate Registry allowing access to a deceased person's assets.

Intestate – When a person has died without leaving a valid will.

Probate – The right to deal with a deceased person's estate.

Testator – The person who has written and left the will.

Will – A document setting out decisions made by a person about how their estate is to be managed and distributed after their death.

When someone makes a will, during their lifetime it remains a confidential document. After their death, and once the will has been proved (meaning that the estate has been distributed), the will becomes a public document. If someone dies intestate and a relative subsequently applies for probate, a grant of administration is issued – this is also public information.

Finding Wills

The index of wills and administrations (grants of representations issued, sometimes called admons, for short) for England and Wales is called the National Probate Calendar. At present these calendars cover almost all of the twentieth century, up to 1996. A calendar entry itself, even without a copy of the will, can be quite informative. Usual information includes:

• The full name of the deceased
• Their address
• The exact date of death
• Place of death
• To whom probate was granted (and relationship to deceased, if a spouse, or their occupation, if not)
• Date that probate was granted
• Place (Probate Sub-Registry) where probate was granted
• The value of the estate

The following extract, from the calendar of 1924, illustrates this:

BAXTER Fanny of the Manor House Barlby **Yorkshire** (wife of William Baxter) died 12 March 1924 Probate **York** 28 April to George Henry Stott retired surveyor's assistant. Effects £45.

BAXTER Fanny of Wisbech Saint Peter **Cambridgeshire** (wife of Thomas Baxter) died 4 July 1924 Probate **Peterborough** 31 July to William James Fysh railway engine driver Francis Robert Fysh groom and James Short Fredrick Fysh railway coalman. Effects £561 14s.

BAXTER Frederick of Central -road Leiston **Suffolk** died 8 November 1923 Probate **London** 4 January to Kate Rowland (wife of Ernest Rowland). Effects £154 15s. 5d.

BAXTER Frederick of the Well Woking **Surrey** died 2 April 1921 Probate **London** 6 February to Agnes Baxter widow and Herbert Leonard Collman librarian. Effects £30550 0s. 4d. Former Grant P.R. July 1921.

BAXTER Frederick Arthur of Yardington Whitchurch **Shropshire** died 24 September 1924 Administration **Shrewsbury** 16 October to Thomas William Baxter newsagent and tobacconist. Effects £951 12s. 4d.

Extract from a probate calendar from 1924. (© *Crown Copyright*)

There is no calendar, as such, for wills from 1996 onward, only online indexes, which are searchable only by surname and year of death. Entries show only the following information:

• Surname and first names of the deceased
• Date that probate was granted

- Date of death
- Document type (whether grant and will or grant only)
- The registry at which probate was issued

Calendars can be searched and viewed on a few sites online:

The official government service is provided by the Probate Service Index to Wills and Administrations – **https://probate search.service.gov.uk 1858–1996**. This is not a searchable index as such, but you can search for an entry on a range of pages in a particular year, which will result in digital images of the pages of the original calendar for you to view, copy or download.

For example, if you type in the surname Atkinson and the year of death 1959, you will land at the first page of the index where this surname is featured. You can then scroll through the pages searching for a particular entry. There is also an option to go back to the previous year or forward to the next year if you are not sure of the exact year of death. Also bear in mind that probate may have been granted at least a year or two after the death. This, therefore, is not a searchable index as such as it doesn't find the exact entry and searching by a range of dates is not possible – it is simply the equivalent of handing you the correct book to look through.

1996–Present: this is fully searchable by name and year and gives the limited search results shown above.

Soldiers' Wills: You can search for wills of any British soldiers who died in service up to 1986.

Probate calendars can also be searched at district probate registries in the following locations in England and Wales:

- Birmingham
- Brighton
- Bristol

Service

Find a will

Wills and Probate 1996 to present	Wills and Probate 1858 – 1996	Soldier's Wills

Search for the will or probate of any person in the UK who died in or after 1996

Surname

eg Smith

Year of death

eg 1996

Search   Advanced search

The search page at https://probatesearch.service.gov.uk.

- Cardiff
- Ipswich
- Leeds (note there is no public access to these indexes: apply for copies of wills by post – see below)
- Liverpool
- London (Principal Probate Registry)
- Manchester
- Newcastle
- Oxford
- Sheffield
- Winchester

There are also a few part-time sub-registries in some districts, but a number of these have been closed in recent years due to restructuring within the department.

Probate registries are classed as courts, and current addresses and contact details for all of the above can be found either by searching by place name or by using the search term 'probate' on the following site: https://courttribunalfinder.service.gov. uk/search.

Ancestry.co.uk has a fully searchable index by name of the National Probate Calendar up to 1966. FindMyPast.co.uk also has searchable calendars up to 1959 (in the Births, Marriages and Deaths category).

Copies of probate calendars for the early part of the twentieth century (up to around 1943) on microfiche/film or in books are available to search at a number of main repositories and libraries including:

- Guildhall Library, London: www.cityoflondon.gov.uk/things-to-do/guildhall-library
- The National Archives, Kew: www.nationalarchives.gov.uk
- The Society of Genealogists Library, London: www.sog.org.uk
- Latter Day Saints Family History Centres in the UK: https://familysearch.org/locations
- County Record Offices and Libraries

What a Will Might Contain

Older wills did not have a set format and the content varies a great deal. Sometimes relatives are mentioned by relationship only – for example: 'I leave all of my property and assets to each of my surviving children in equal shares.' Usually, however, the names are given, in addition to the relationship. This is particularly useful in identifying which children survived parents, and also the married names of daughters. Be aware, however, that not all children are necessarily beneficiaries of the estate of a parent and sometimes a person's estate might be left to a friend or a charity, even though there are surviving children. In addition to the names of relatives and their relationship to the deceased, a will can contain other interesting details such as the location and size of property and land and descriptions of family heirlooms.

Obtaining a Copy of a Will

Online

You can now apply online for a copy of any will or grant from 1858 onwards via the official government website: www.gov.uk/wills-probate-inheritance/searching-for-probate-records. Copies cost £10 and are delivered electronically as pdf versions; this usually takes a few days.

In person

If you are able to visit the Principal Probate Registry in London in person you can order copies of wills and grants here. This court used to offer a 'same-day service' but this has been discontinued and the documents can now be collected after three working days. The address is:

Principal Registry of the Family Division
7th Floor
42–49 High Holborn
First Avenue House
Holborn
London WC1V 6NP
Website:
londonpersonalapplicationsenquiries@hmcts.gsi.gov.uk
Tel.: 0207 421 8509 or 0207 421 8500

By post

You can apply for a copy of a will or grant by post by completing application form PA1S (see link below for download address) and sending it, together with the fee of £10, to:

Leeds District Probate Registry
Postal Searches and Copies Department
York House
York Place
Leeds LS1 2BA

Website:
http://hmctsformfinder.justice.gov.uk/courtfinder/forms/pa001s-eng.pdf
Email: LeedsDPRenquiries@hmcts.gsi.gov.uk
Tel. 0113 389 6133

Case Study – Warren

Warren wanted to find his cousin Lyndsay after returning to the UK following twelve years working in Canada. 'I teach engineering,' says Warren, 'and when I was offered a job in Canada twelve years ago I jumped at the chance. Being recently divorced I was keen to escape and make a fresh start. I kept in touch with my parents, of course, but didn't worry too much about other family members because mum and dad kept me updated with news.'

Warren's father died after he had been in Canada for ten years. At first his mother coped, but she soon started to develop memory problems and then had a fall. Warren decided to take extended unpaid leave to care for her. 'Being an only child, I felt that it was my responsibility to be there with mum.'

Adjusting to life back in the UK was difficult for Warren but he was pleased to catch up with friends. One person he really wanted to see, however, was Lyndsay, the daughter of his mother's late brother Bill. When Uncle Bill had died seven years previously, Warren flew over from Canada for the funeral. This had been the last time he saw Lyndsay. 'We chatted for a long time at the wake,' says Warren, 'reminiscing about the times we had spent together as children. Lyndsay was my only cousin and around the same age so we had been like brother and sister as kids.'

Warren decided to find Lyndsay, but discovered that it was not as easy as he had hoped. 'I went to the library, joined Facebook, fiddled around on the internet for hours and asked everyone I could think of but Lyndsay was very elusive!'

The breakthrough came when Warren found the will of Lyndsay's mother, Sheila. Warren told me that his Uncle Bill and Auntie Sheila had lived in a small Northumberland village. When Warren looked for Sheila on the electoral register, she was not there. A death record was found but, disappointingly, Sheila's death was registered by an unrelated person, suggesting that Lyndsay had not been available at the time. He then searched for Sheila's will and luckily, when this arrived, it was quite detailed. The main beneficiary of the will was Lyndsay, with a different surname and an address in the Channel Islands.

Warren wrote to the address and received a call from his excited cousin a few days later. Lyndsay told him how she had moved to Jersey to work in a bank there six years previously. She had married a colleague and was now settled in Jersey. 'It's wonderful,' says Warren. 'We have visited each other and I'm now great friends with Lyndsay's husband, Bob. It feels like having a new family.'

Wills in Scotland

Indexes to wills and grants in Scotland (excluding Orkney and Shetland) up to 1925 are searchable and available for download on the Scotland's People website: www.scotlandspeople.gov.uk (registration and fees apply). Index entries list the name, title, occupation, residence of the deceased, the court location and the date.

For detailed information about wills in Scotland from 1925 to 1999 visit the website of the National Records of Scotland (NRS) at www.nrscotland.gov.uk/research/guides/wills-and-testaments.

In brief, you will need to either visit the NRS or get someone to undertake a search and order documents on your behalf. You should know the name, residence of the deceased and when they died in order to search for a will or grant. A reader's ticket will be required to gain access to the search room. The address is:

National Records of Scotland
2 Princes Street
Edinburgh
Scotland EH1 3YY
Tel. 0131 535 1314

Wills in Northern Ireland

Will Calendars for Northern Ireland for the three district probate registries of Armagh, Belfast and Londonderry are available to search online at the website of the Public Record Office for Northern Ireland: www.proni.gov.uk. The information on the calendars is quite detailed and includes name, date of death, place of death, occupation, date of grant, where probate was granted and to whom. Transcribed copies of wills up to 1909 for Belfast and 1918 for Armagh are also available through this site. There are no transcribed copies of wills for the twentieth century for Londonderry available online.

Copies of wills proved more than seven years ago are available to order in person, by post or by email from the PRONI. The address is:

Public Record Office for Northern Ireland
2 Titanic Boulevard
Titanic Quarter
Belfast BT3 9HQ
Northern Ireland
Email: proni@dcalni.gov.uk
Tel. 028 90 534800

Chapter 6

NEWSPAPERS, PHOTOS AND FILM

Newspaper archives can hold valuable and in many cases unique information about the lives of our ancestors and the places in which they lived. Within the pages of newspapers, both national and local, we can discover details of the daily lives of ordinary people. Behind the headlines of national affairs, famous (and infamous) people, major events and gossip of the day, there can be found a treasure trove that may have been trivial in its day but is now an account, frozen in time, of the everyday lives of our ancestors. You might find:

• Family announcements of births/christenings, engagements/ marriages, birthdays, anniversaries or deaths/funerals
• Obituaries for anyone well known in the local area or who held a position of importance
• Articles concerning events that would have affected your ancestors, giving context to your research, and perhaps finding references to ancestors who were there
• Legal notices concerning crimes, court cases, punishment, civil disputes and more
• Letters – 'Letters to the Editor' contain the actual words, phrases and views of the people who wrote them
• Sports reports – team events, local sportsmen and officials, tournaments and awards
• Advertisements – local advertising for small businesses in the days before the internet

It is important to remember that articles about events reported in newspapers were unofficial accounts and may be biased or even untruthful. Also, they might not be followed up in subsequent issues.

Local newspaper articles can be extremely detailed. Each week enough 'news' had to be reported to fill a paper and, in the absence of scandal or disaster, stories about everyday trivia from school sports days and council meetings to cake sales and parking problems were often examined and described in detail.

Here is the text from a typical local newspaper report about a funeral written in the mid-1950s (names have been changed):

Funeral of the late Mrs Wilson

The funeral took place of local resident Mrs Nellie Wilson (76) on Friday last. She died the previous Thursday at her home in Rose Street after a fall down the stairs. Mrs Wilson, widow of the late Geoffrey Wilson, was the secretary of the local gardening group and was well known for her beautiful dahlias.

The Reverend W. Cross spoke of Nellie's devotion to her family and her love of the outdoors. Mourners were led by her sister, Mrs Gladys Toogood, who travelled from Cumbria to bid farewell. Nieces Miss Diane Toogood and Mrs Caroline Pratt were also present, as was her nephew, Mr Toby Toogood. Nellie's daughter, Mrs Brenda Collins, was unable to attend as she is heavy with child and could not endure the journey from Exeter where her husband is working at present. Mrs Collins sent a large floral tribute with a note saying 'Mum, I will miss you so much. Rest in peace. Your heartbroken daughter, Bren x.'

Pall-bearers and other mourners included some of Nellie's fellow gardeners, Mrs Paula Hicks, Mr Ron Hatch, Mrs Winnie Goodridge, Mr James Collier, Mrs Maggie Ross and Mrs Daisy Tindall. Nellie was laid to rest with her late husband Geoffrey in the leafy west corner of the church cemetery. Most of the women gathered at the graveside were in a distressed state after the interment. A wake with plentiful tea and sandwiches took place in the village hall at lunch time, where many photographs of Nellie throughout her life were displayed.

Mrs Ross, who now takes over as secretary of the gardening club, said that Nellie's allotment is now available for rent and applications, care of the village hall post box, would be welcome.

This report not only gives an insight into Mrs Wilson's popularity but also names many of her relatives.

Local newspapers also offer a provincial perspective on national events and reports can feature ancestors who lived in the area. This report, about the Jarrow March of 1936 from Tyneside to London in protest at the lack of jobs, was featured in the *Nottingham Evening Post*. The town was a stopover point for the 200 or so men who were undertaking the march, which took almost a month. The article mentions a local hostel where the men stayed and its proprietor, Mr T. Boot.

Extract from the *Nottingham Post*, 1936. (© *Local World Limited/Trinity Mirror*)

Where to Find Newspapers

Most libraries subscribe to some local and national newspapers for readers to consult. Usually, in branch libraries, copies of newspapers are discarded after a period of time due to lack of storage space. Most large city and county libraries, however, hold hard copy or microfilm archives of local paper titles, sometimes dating back to the 1800s and beyond. Before digitisation, electronic indexing and the internet, established national papers (and some regional and county ones too) had printed indexes that were issued annually, sometimes with cumulative volumes. For smaller local titles, where there was no official index, library staff sometimes kept card indexes or clippings files of stories relating to local places and people. Hampshire County Library, for example, holds a comprehensive archive of the *Hampshire Chronicle* on microfilm and in hard copy from 1772 to date with indexes for later years. In addition to hard copy indexes, there are indexes on CD ROM for a few national titles, including the Official Index to The Times, 1906–1980, which is available in many large libraries. Individual newspaper companies can also hold their own archives, which are often comprehensive but sometimes there are access restrictions due to the age and condition of the original editions.

For many years the British Library had a special newspaper library site at Colindale, London, with thousands of international, national, regional and local newspapers in hard copy and on microfilm, but this facility closed permanently in 2013. The printed newspaper archives were moved to storage at the British Library's Boston Spa site in West Yorkshire while the vast microfilm collection was moved to the new British Library Newsroom at the St Pancras site in London, which opened in April 2014. Read more about the facilities, collections and access to the 34,000 titles from the UK and around the world on this British Library guide: www.bl.uk/collection-guides/newspapers.

Newspapers Online

Until recently public access to the contents of historical newspapers was limited. Unless you knew the area in which an event took place, the publication in which it was reported and the approximate date, it was not possible to locate information without spending hours in libraries engaged in painstaking searches through old volumes or microfilms. In fact, you had to be fairly sure that something of value about your ancestor was contained in one of these volumes before you even started a search.

Thanks to technological advances and investment in major digitisation programmes in recent years, it is now possible to search newspaper archives and view digital images of the print archives. Individual newspaper websites often have a search facility, some going back just a few years and some more than a century. Almost all national and local newspapers are involved in some way in digital archiving, although some will charge for access to images of original archives. To identify titles, websites and history of newspapers worldwide, visit www.online newspapers.com. This is a fabulous, free facility, with the newspapers arranged by continent, country and then alphabetically by title, linking to thousands of newspaper websites from around the world.

British Newspaper Archive

The British Library, in partnership with brightsolid, the company behind findmypast.co.uk, is undertaking an ambitious ten-year project to digitise around 40 million pages from thousands of local and regional newspapers. The results of this project are being released as available and already there are already almost 500 titles up to 1959 that are fully searchable with digital images of the original papers. Indexing so many titles and pages has been made possible by optical character recognition technology, which scans the pages electronically, selecting words and characters for indexing. As there is no manual checking or correction, there are inevitably omissions and errors due to poor print quality or condition of the original material. Despite this, however, this archive opens up potentially hitherto unknown information about British people and places going back more than a century.

To access this collection, from the homepage www.findmypast.co.uk click on Search, then Newspapers & Periodicals, then British Newspapers 1710–1953. To search for an individual, use the 'Who' search field to enter a first name and last name. You can then narrow your search by date, place, county, newspaper title and article type. It is worth pointing out that it was not common to use first names so much in the past as it is today. Even lengthy articles could be written about individuals using only their initials and surname – for example, 'Mr A.W. Palmer voted new chair of district Rotary Club'. Also, in the early part of the century there was a trend, now considered very old-fashioned, for a married woman to be known by her husband's name: Mr and Mrs Frederick Price, for example. Fascinating local trivia giving a snapshot of the daily lives of our relatives and ancestors can be uncovered in minutes, such as this extract from the *Portsmouth Evening News* from 1934:

ST. MARGARET'S WHIST

The series of Tuesday evening drives continue to be popular at St. Margaret's Institute, Haslemere Road. There was a good attendance last night when Mr. Chalmers again officiated as M.C. Among the prize-winners were Mesdames Chalmers, Cullingford and Trim, Misses North and Reade, and Mr. H. Cawdrey. Refreshments were superintended by Mesdames Caudrey and Harvey.

A report of a local whist drive in the Hampshire area, 1934. (© *Portsmouth News*)

The British Newspaper Archive is accessible as part of a normal Find My Past subscription or on a pay per view basis. However, this collection can be accessed for free at the British Library and at almost all main county and city libraries.

The Times Digital Archive (1785–1985) is a fully searchable facsimile of every issue of *The Times* over this 200-year period. Access to this is free in the British Library Reading Rooms in London (you will need to register and obtain a pass) and at many county and university libraries throughout the country. With some library memberships the archive can also be accessed from home through your account. There are also extended editions of the archive available (to 2009 at the time of writing). For more information see: http://gale.cengage.co.uk/times.aspx.

Photographs
One advantage that the twentieth century has over research into earlier times is that there are more likely to be images of your relatives and ancestors. Your older relatives may have photo albums or maybe you inherited boxes of pictures, which is a great start. However, the two main problems with having family photos are identification and preservation.

Identifying who is who, where they were and when is essential. If you don't know who the people in your photographs are, then future generations don't have a hope of finding out, so start now with recording as much information as possible (without writing on the back). Show your photos to all the relatives you can think of, study them closely, try to work out which ones are of the same people and estimate their ages and the date. Write down not just the names of people in the photos but also how they were related and on which side of the family (maternal or paternal) – just writing 'Granny Elsie' or 'Great Aunt Mabel' probably won't be helpful to future generation. If you're not sure about the identity of someone in a photo, take a guess but place a question mark next to the name. For comprehensive information about finding, dating, analysing and understanding family photographs, Jane Shrimpton's book, *Tracing Your Ancestors through Family Photographs* is an invaluable resource.

Preserving the photographs we have is important, but many people do this incorrectly. Putting pictures in a frame behind glass is not a good way to keep them as they can become faded and damaged. Scan photographs at the highest density (dpi) that you can to preserve as much detail as possible, but apart from this avoid handling original prints. Old photographs should be kept in an acid-free environment to prevent deterioration, either in sleeves, albums or archive boxes; don't use ordinary photo albums if you can avoid it. There are a couple of good websites describing the basic care of old photographs: www.national archives.gov.uk/documents/archivesconservation_photo.pdf and www.hintsandthings.co.uk/workshop/photographs.htm.

As well as your own photos, and those belonging to people in your family, it is possible that there are images of your relatives and ancestors in public, private or corporate collections. Throughout their lives your relatives will probably have had their photograph taken at events, to mark occasions and at locations where they lived and worked.

We have already covered the subject of newspaper articles, and it is a great bonus if such articles have pictures to accompany them. However, in addition to the grainy newspaper picture, there may well be an original copy in the library or archive of the newspaper company. If the paper is no longer published the archives, including the photo library, may be in a repository so it is worth exploring Discovery, the catalogue of the National Archives, which details not just records held at Kew but also resources held at 2,500 archives across the country – this facility is searchable by keyword, with descriptions of 32 million records. Some documents and pictures are available to download, although there may be a charge for this. The internet has millions of images from around the country and the globe with more being added all the time. There are collections like that of Historic England, for example – https://historicengland.org.uk/images-books/archive – which has over a million photos, plans and drawings of places around the country. These are mostly pictures of buildings and landscapes, but often include people who lived, visited or worked there. Local libraries, parish councils and village community groups may also have records and photos of people who lived in the area. Companies, organisations, sports teams, clubs and social or specialist interest groups often have collections of records and photographs of events through the years. Thanks to social media, the sharing of photographs has never been easier. You don't need to know or meet someone to see their photographs and you can also share your photographs with others. Groups on social media sites like Facebook and Friends Reunited relating to particular locations are popular and finding photos of people and places at a specific time can be as easy as posting an appeal. For example, Romsey Revisited is a closed Facebook group for anyone with a connection to this Hampshire town. Members chat about 'the old days', post pictures, ask for information, share news, trace relatives or friends and generally reminisce about the town and people who lived there.

Think about where your ancestor lived, where they worked, what their hobbies were and any events they might have attended and you may discover hitherto unknown photographs to add to your collection.

Film and Video

The dawn of the twentieth century coincided with the birth of film. The first motion picture cameras were invented in the 1890s, in time to capture a handful of events in the last years of Queen Victoria's life. There survive a few short, stilted, silent films showing the monarch, mostly at state occasions in horse-drawn carriages. There is also footage of her funeral procession in 1901, featuring not just the grand cortège but thousands of those present on the day – relatives, staff, guests and members of her adoring public. The first public showing of a moving film in the UK took place in 1896 at what would later become the Regent Street Cinema in London. French inventors the Lumière brothers introduced Britain to the first film shown from a manual projector called a cinematograph, to a small, awestruck audience who had each paid a shilling to see the 40-second film.

Production companies started springing up, such as Mitchell & Kenyon of Blackburn, which was formed in 1897. Mostly these companies captured the daily lives of ordinary people, such as workers leaving factories and families on Sunday walks in the streets where they lived. People at fairs, parades, sporting events, national celebrations and seaside resorts were regularly captured on foot, bicycles, public transport, boats and sometimes in the newly invented motor cars. Although factual films were most popular, short fiction films were also emerging, with simple plots, that were shot in the first studios. Amateur actors and extras took part in early films and their names started to appear on film credits. The profession of acting developed, as did the concept of 'film stars' such as Greta Garbo and Charlie Chaplin. Equity, the trade union for actors, was established in 1930.

Pathé News, originating from a French company set up in the late Victorian era, was established in the UK in 1910 as British Pathé. Early footage of notable events includes the coronation of King George V in 1911 and the Epsom Derby of 1913 at which suffragette Emily Davison was killed. Pathé has a substantial collection of films from the First World War, although not all were catalogued so the identity and location of the soldiers are sometimes unknown. In the 1930s the Pathé newsreel format started to become popular and short Pathé News films were shown at cinemas all over the country up until the 1970s before the main popular film and during the interlude. There is an extensive collection of film shot during the Second World War, both at home and abroad, including Dunkirk and the D-Day landings. My aunt, Mary Newman, is shown and named in a short film titled 'Heroes All', on a visit to Buckingham Palace in 1941 to collect her George Medal, which was awarded for bravery as a student nurse during the Southampton Blitz. Explore www.britishpathe.com to search films and view for free (there is a charge to download videos). Other sites worth exploring for film archive are MovieTone – www.movietone.com – and Britain on Film from the British Film Institute – www.bfi.org.uk/britain-on-film.

Amateur film clubs whose members started using home cine cameras were popular from the mid-1920s right up until the early 1980s, when VHS video was introduced. Although formats and technology changed a great deal during that time, the surviving reels of film, which can now be converted to digital formats, provide an insight into the working and middle classes of the mid-twentieth century. Family gatherings such as christenings and weddings, adults at work and leisure and children at play were captured by enthusiasts who loved their hobby and perhaps understood its importance for future generations. Some of these films were sadly lost, damaged or destroyed but many do survive in family homes, private collections and public archives. Read *Amateur Film: Meaning and Practice, 1927–1977* by Heather Norris Nicholson for more information on this fascinating subject.

Some films survive as part of public collections, such as the Wessex Film Archive: www3.hants.gov.uk/wfsa.htm; originally a private company, it is now part of the Hampshire Record Office and holds 36,000 film and sound recordings relating to Hampshire and the surrounding counties. The British Library also has an extensive collection of sound recordings and moving images spanning more than a century from all over the world; visit www.bl.uk for general information on the collection or http://cadensa.bl.uk/cgi-bin/webcat to search the sound and moving image catalogue.

Information about film and video would not be complete

without a mention of YouTube – www.youtube.com – a global phenomenon now owned by Google. It began in 2005 as a way for people to share and view videos, but the site now has more than a billion registered users, from individuals, groups and small companies to large corporations. Millions of historical videos have been uploaded and searches can be made by keyword. A word of warning: because anyone can upload videos, sometimes copyright has been infringed, editing can change original film and some videos are simply false or incorrectly titled.

Chapter 7

CONFLICT AND DEFENCE

The two world wars dominate our perception of British conflict in the twentieth century. Yet the century started and ended with conflicts involving British forces, with military involvement somewhere in the world consistently in between; in fact there was only one calendar year, 1968, in which no British service personnel were killed on active service. From the Second Boer War (1899–1902) to the Kosovo War (1998–1999), there were interventions, confrontations, civil wars, occupations and liberations continuing throughout; in fact, there has not been one whole year since 1914 in which no British forces were involved in any kind of conflict.

It isn't just fighting that occupies our armed forces, however. Peacekeeping duties, humanitarian aid, training, updating and preparing for conflict keeps our service personnel constantly busy.

British armed forces comprise the three main services: the Army, the Royal Navy (including the Royal Marines) and the Royal Air Force, plus volunteer reserve forces. Each force has a hierarchy that comprises, for example, regiments, battalions, squadrons, brigades and divisions. You can read more about the structure of British armed forces, during the First World War and today, on the following websites: the Long, Long Trail – www.1914–1918.net; the Great War – www.greatwar.co.uk; and Armed Forces UK – www.armedforces.co.uk/Europeandefence/ edcountries/countryuk.htm.

Conscription

Of all the British conflicts, the First and Second World Wars are the ones that are most likely to have involved at least one relative or ancestor from almost every family. This is because, unlike the regular armed forces, which are made up of personnel who choose to enter the forces as a profession, in both world wars there was conscription (the compulsory enlistment of soldiers).

There was no conscription at the start of the First World War but the government recognised early on that the army needed more manpower. Volunteers were called for and within a few months over a million men had joined up. This wasn't enough, however, and with casualties rising and volunteer numbers falling, the National Registration Act was introduced. From January 1916 all single men aged between 18 and 41 were enlisted. Exemption was only allowed on health grounds and for certain professions such as the clergy or those undertaking important work for the war effort. Within a few months, when the supply of fit, single men ran short, conscription was extended to married men.

At the outbreak of the Second World War in September 1939 the National Service (Armed Forces) Act was quickly passed, imposing conscription upon all men aged 18 to 41 with a few exceptions, including medical exemption, work in vital occupations such as doctors, clergy and police officers, and conscientious objectors. By 1942 the age of compulsory conscription had risen to 51 and single females between the ages of 20 and 30 were also called up.

Tribunals

Many of the men who were called up applied for exemption from conscription for various reasons, including domestic hardship, business commitments, health problems and on moral or religious grounds. These appeals were dealt with by more than

2,000 local Military Service Tribunals and by the end of 1916 almost 800,000 men had made applications for exemption. If initial tribunals dismissed an application, an appeal could be made to one of the eighty-three County Appeal Tribunals. Very few local appeal tribunal records have survived; after the war the government instructed local boards to destroy the records due to their sensitive nature, although some for the First World War do survive at County Record Offices. In addition, many tribunals were covered in newspapers. There is only one full set of County Appeal Tribunal records and this is for the county of Middlesex. Documents relating to 11,000 tribunals are held by the National Archives. In 2014, following a project to digitise and index all of the papers, the series was launched as a fully searchable set. It is held in the MH47 series and can be searched by name via the Discovery Catalogue. Read this National Archives guide for more information: www.nationalarchives. gov.uk/conscription-appeals.

Army Service Records
Most of the servicemen and women who served in the two world wars were enlisted into the army. More than 6 million personnel, the majority of them men, served in the First World War in some capacity. Unfortunately, a number of army service records kept at the War Office were later destroyed by air raid damage, but almost 3 million records survived intact. Some documents were damaged but later microfilmed and some records of service were reconstructed from pension records. Thanks to preservation, microfilming and digitisation, there is around a 40 per cent chance that the service record of a soldier who served between 1914 and 1920 survives in some form, although many are damaged or incomplete to some extent and some are only in the form of transcripts. If one of these records relates to your ancestor, what information can you hope to discover?

The basic information includes:

- Name
- Age in years and months
- Date of attestation (enlistment)
- Birth year, country and county
- Country of residence
- Death date (if during service)
- Service number (i.e. regimental number)
- Documents series - WO 363 (service records) for example
- Rank
- Regiment
- Unit/Battalion

If an enlistment form survives (such as the one below) you may find further information, including:

- Physical description (including, height, eye colour and tattoos)
- Occupation
- Marital status and next of kin
- Names of children and their ages
- Any previous service history
- Religion
- Signature
- Pension details and any additional correspondence

Images of surviving records and transcriptions of key information can be searched, viewed and downloaded on both Ancestry under Military Records and Find My Past under a record set titled British Army Service Records 1914–1920. Read the following National Archives research guide for more information about First World War records: www.nationalarchives.gov.uk/first-world-war.

Service Records – Second World War and Beyond
All armed service records from 1920 onwards, including those of Second World War service personnel, remain in the custody of the Ministry of Defence.

Extract from the attestation record of a soldier, 1915. (© *The National Archives WO363/30972/893; reproduced by courtesy of Ancestry.com*)

Veterans can request a copy of their own army service record (including those from 1941 onwards) from the MOD Army Personnel Centre in Glasgow by completing a Data Protection Subject Access Request (SAR) Form 1694.

Extracts from records of deceased army personnel who died more than twenty-five years ago can be provided upon application for a fee of £30 if a copy of a death certificate is supplied, unless death was in service (the fee is waived for the spouse, civil partner or parent of the deceased soldier). The information that is disclosed will usually contain:

- Name
- Place of birth
- Date of birth
- Date of joining the service
- Rank
- Service number
- Regiment/corps
- Units served in, with dates and locations
- Dates of this service and the locations of those units
- Date of death if this was in service
- Date of leaving service
- Conduct medals (e.g. Long Service and Good Conduct Medal)
- Gallantry awards

All application forms and an explanation of the procedure for obtaining copies of service records (including those for Royal Air Force and Royal Navy personnel) are available on the following website: www.gov.uk/guidance/requests-for-personal-data-and-service-records (formerly Veterans UK). The Army Personnel Centre in Glasgow can also be contacted in writing or by telephone:

APC Glasgow
Kentigern House
65 Brown Street
GLASGOW G2 8EX
Tel. 0141 224 3600 (general enquiries)

Unit War Diaries and Operations Record Books

If you know, or can discover, the army unit (battalion, corps, division, etc.) that your relative served in, this can be an additional source of information about where they were and what they were doing overseas during both world wars. All army units kept a record of daily events, which can include location, operations, movements, successes, losses and map references. These diaries do not often contain information about individual soldiers unless they were killed or, for example, committed an act of exceptional bravery. Many of these diaries are held in the WO95 series at the National Archives, although they are not indexed and only some have been digitised as part of an ongoing project – read more about unit diaries, including details of how to access and search them, on this helpful web page: www.nationalarchives.gov.uk /first-world-war/centenary-unit-war-diaries.

The Royal Air Force kept a similar set of records – known as operation record books – for each squadron, although only those for the Second World War survive and are kept in the AIR27 series. Only part of this series has been digitised. The following guide explains holdings, access and examples of content: www.national archives.gov.uk/help-with-your-research/research-guides/raf-operations-record-books-1939-1945.

Records of Medals and Awards

A number of medals were awarded during the First World War and all servicemen were eligible to receive at least one campaign medal if they served overseas. As medal rolls for both the army and navy are complete and indexed, you will almost certainly find a record of medals awarded to your relatives if they served overseas.

For the army, around 5.5 million medal index cards are held in the WO (War Office) series at the National Archives, each containing the name, rank, regiment, service number and the medals awarded. Sometimes details of places and dates of service and other remarks were recorded. You can search the catalogue for medal cards and digital images of the originals are available to purchase and download (the cost is currently £3.30). However, transcriptions of the card contents can be viewed on Find My Past in the British Army medal index cards 1914–1920 series and records of medals can also be located on Ancestry under UK WWI Service Medal and Award Rolls, 1914–1920 – medal index card records found here are high resolution, colour digital images, like this one, which includes an entry for my maternal grandfather, Edward Newman:

Name.		Corps.	Rank.	Regtl. No.
		Hamps R.	*Pte.*	*2553.*
NEWMAN.	# — " —		— " —	*240978.*
Edward. A. F.				

Medal.	Roll.	Page.		Remarks.
VICTORY				
BRITISH	*R/1/103* *a*	*76.*		
STAR				
IND. GS. AFGN. NWFF. 1919 (ROLL # *16680 – 118)*				
Theatre of War first served in				
Date of entry therein				K. 1880

The First World War medal card of Edward A.F. Newman. (© *The National Archives WO372/14/206422; reproduced by courtesy of Ancestry.com*)

There are also indexes on Ancestry for more distinguished medals including the Victoria Cross, which was awarded to just 627 recipients for 'valour in the face of the enemy' during the First World War. Many of these entries contain photographs of the recipient and, if they were killed in action, pictures of their grave or memorial. Read the following guide for more details of campaign and service medals: www.nationalarchives.gov.uk /help-with-your-research/research-guides/british-military-campaign-and-service-medals.

Casualties

Sadly, you are more likely to find records for an ancestor if they were killed in action or died in service.

The **Commonwealth War Graves Commission** is responsible for the care of cemeteries and memorials worldwide that commemorate the 1.7 million people who died in the two world wars, both service personnel and civilians. The Commission's website – www.cwgc.org – has a search facility that can be narrowed down by name, date, conflict, force, country of death, unit, rank and regiment. You can also search by service number, if you know it. In addition to the name of the deceased (which may only be an initial and surname), the result may include details such as:

• Rank
• Service number
• Date of death
• Age
• Regiment/Service
• Cemetery
• Grave/Memorial reference

You can also print a certificate, which many include additional information such as next of kin.

Other records of service casualties online include Findmypast.co.uk's National Roll Of The Great War 1914–1918 and Ancestry.co.uk's UK, Soldiers Died in the Great War, 1914–1919. There are many other collections, which you can find via the National Archives guide to digitised First World War Records – www.nationalarchives.gov.uk/first-world-war/centenary-digitised-records – and its guide to researching Second World War records: www.nationalarchives.gov.uk/help-with-your-research/research-guides/second-world-war.

Records available include:

Army:
- Prisoner of war interview reports 1914–1918
- Women's Army Auxiliary Corps service records 1917–1920
- Household Cavalry soldiers' service records 1799–1920
- British Army nurses' service records 1914–1918
- British Army war diaries 1914–1922
- Prisoners of War 1939–1945 – British Army held in German Territories

Royal Air Force:
- Royal Air Force officers' service records 1918–1919
- Women's Royal Air Force service records 1918–1920

Navy:
- Royal Navy ratings' service records 1853–1923
- Royal Navy officers' service records 1756–1931
- Royal Naval Air Service officers' service records 1906–1918
- Women's Royal Naval service records 1917–1919
- Volunteer Reserve service records 1903–1922
- Royal Naval Division service records 1914–1919
- Royal Navy officers' service record cards and files c.1840–c.1920
- Royal Naval Reserve service records 1860–1955
- Royal Marines service records 1842–1925

The **Armed Forces Memorial Roll of Honour** commemorates all members of the armed forces who have died in military service since the end of the Second World War. It is updated quarterly. You can search by name on the AMF website – www.afm-veterans-uk.info – where you can also print off a certificate containing details of their service in the armed forces.

Memorials
If your ancestor's name is commemorated on one of the thousands of memorials that stand in cities, towns and villages throughout Britain, you may wish to visit the memorial to pay your respects. You can look for memorials online – many have photographs and lists of names.

The website www.roll-of-honour.com details memorials by county, many with photographs, and also includes many overseas memorials and rolls of honour. The Imperial War Museum has an ongoing project, called the UK War Memorials Archive, to record and transcribe individual names on memorials around the country. Currently there are details for more than 66,000 memorials. Visit the website for updates on the project and to search for memorials or the names recorded on them: www.iwm.org.uk/about-iwm/projects-and-partnerships/uk-war-memorials-archive. The War Memorials Trust – www.war memorials. org – was established to help protect and conserve memorials, and War Memorials Online – www.warmemorials online.org.uk – aims to build information on the location and condition of memorials and record images submitted by volunteers.

Another interesting and helpful website is www.inmemories. com. More than 3,500 war cemeteries, communal graves and local churchyards across Belgium and France that contain the remains of fallen Allied personnel, or memorials to them, are being painstakingly recorded, photographed and catalogued.

Museums

There are a number of museums around the country dedicated to the armed services. Although you may not find records in museums about individual members of the armed services, you can explore stories and artefacts that will expand your knowledge and understanding of various military campaigns and how people lived while in the services.

The Imperial War Museum – www.iwm.org.uk – has collections, exhibitions, artefacts and research material that bring to life the wars in Britain and the Commonwealth from 1914 to the present. There are five museums in the IWM family: London, North (Manchester), Duxford (Cambridgeshire), the Churchill War Rooms (Whitehall) and HMS *Belfast* (River Thames).

Each of the armed services also has its own museum and the websites all offer some guidance on military family history research:

- The National Army Museum in Chelsea: www.nam.ac.uk
- The RAF Museum in London and Shropshire: www.rafmuseum. org.uk
- The National Museum of the Royal Navy in Portsmouth: www.nmrn.org.uk

In addition, there are museums for individual regiments. There are 139 military museums across the UK detailed on the website of the Army Museums Ogilby Trust –www.armymuseums.org.uk. This site also features detailed guidance on military ancestor research.

Civilian Stories

Many civilians played a part in both major conflicts of the twentieth century. Women, older men and those who were found unfit for regular service not only took on the jobs of the men who had gone to fight but also fulfilled civilian war roles.

The **Home Guard**, originally named the Local Defence Volunteers, was formed in 1940 as a force to guard coastal areas and factories in a last line of defence against invasion. Although sometimes portrayed by the TV series 'Dad's Army' as a rather inept bunch of amateurs, many in the Home Guard, in fact around 40 per cent, were First World War veterans. They were armed and trained to deal with enemy invasion and also carried out other duties such as the manning of artillery and bomb disposal. There were 1.7 million members in the Home Guard by the end of 1944. More than 1,600 Home Guard soldiers were killed on duty and around 1,000 were awarded medals and commendations for bravery or exceptional service.

The only records available online, unless the soldier was a casualty of war, are those for the Durham Home Guard, which are held in the War Office collection at the National Archives, in series WO 409. Enrolment forms, similar to those used for the regular army, can be viewed and searched on site in Kew, London. The same forms from 1939 to 1945, which have been digitised and indexed, can be searched online and downloaded (cost £3.30) from the Discovery catalogue – see the following guide for more details: www.nationalarchives.gov.uk/help-with-your-research/research-guides/durham-home-guard-records-1939-1945. Please note that these online records relate to the Durham County Home Guard only. Home Guard service records for all other counties and cities are still held by the Ministry of Defence. The procedure and cost for applying for copies of the service records for soldiers is the same as for regular army records (see above). Visit www.gov.uk/guidance/requests-for-personal-data-and-service-records or call 0141 224 3600 for an application form.

Sometimes you can find photographs, letters and surviving papers concerning a local Home Guard unit in county and city record offices. For example, the Hampshire Record Office catalogue includes the following:

• Warnford Platoon, Home Guard (Droxford East Company): outpost duty rotas and platoon orders
• Photograph of members of Bracknell Platoon Home Guard No. 1 Section, 1944. All are named on the reverse and the names include Sergeant Lamb
• Photographic negative of Bishops Waltham LDV members (Local Defence Volunteers, later the Home Guard)

For a fascinating insight into the life of Home Guard soldiers, read Dr Stephen M. Cullen's *In Search of the Real Dad's Army* (Pen & Sword, 2011).

ARP (Civil Defence) Wardens

The ARP (Air Raid Precautions) service was set up in 1937, before the war, when it was first feared that bombing raids might begin. Wardens were recruited and directed by local authorities; some were full-time, paid employees but most were volunteers. Initially most recruits were older men but in 1938 the WRVS was formed so that women could also be involved. The duties of an air raid warden included enforcing the blackout, checking gas masks, supervising and assisting people to shelters, patrolling streets, evacuating dangerous areas, helping to rescue casualties and extinguishing fires. It was a dangerous job and more than 6,000 wardens were killed on duty. One of these wardens was my grandfather, Edward Newman, a First World War veteran; he was aged 47 when he died, and was married with nine children (the youngest being my mother, who was just 2 years old at the time of his death). The Commonwealth War Graves Commission published seven volumes of civilian casualties, including ARP wardens, and entries from these volumes are now searchable online on the Commonwealth War Graves Commission website – www.cwgc.org – and on Ancestry.co.uk in a record set called UK Civilian Deaths, 1939–45. Here is the entry for my grandfather:

NEWMAN, EDWARD ARCHIBALD FRANK, age 47; Air Raid Warden. Son of the late George and Fanny Newman, of Romsey; husband of Ada Florence Newman, of 70 Magnolia Road, Bitterne. 22 June 1942, at A.R.P. Post, 3 Merry Oak.

Entry from *Civilian War Dead in the United Kingdom, 1939–1945.* (*Commonwealth War Graves Commission*)

Copies of local entries are usually held in larger local authority libraries and archives. Entries can also be searched, and a certificate generated for you to print off and frame, on the Commonwealth War Graves Commission website; you can narrow down entries by selecting 'civilian' in the Advanced Search option. If your ARP relative survived the war, there are likely to be records that survive in the archives of the local authority where they worked. In some counties and city boroughs you will find staff records or registration cards giving name, age, address and next of kin. Maps of jurisdiction areas, rotas and correspondence can also form part of the records and sometimes the local ARP would even have its own magazine.

Civilian ancestors who were awarded gallantry medals can be identified on Discovery, the catalogue of the National Archives – http://discovery.nationalarchives.gov.uk. Here I found an entry for my aunt's award in the Home Office records (although her first middle name, Sybil, is spelt incorrectly):

Reference: HO 250/12/493
Description: Case number: 493
Name: Mary Sible Joyce Newman
Age: 18
Occupation: Nurse, Southampton
Brief Summary of Ground for Recommendation: Administered first aid in dangerous conditions at Southampton, [Hampshire] on 23 November 1940
Date: 1941 Feb 4

Read the following guide for help with identifying civilian medals and awards for gallantry: www.nationalarchives.gov.uk/help-with-your-research/research-guides/civilian-gallantry-medals.

The **Women's Land Army** (WLA) was first created in 1917 in an effort to increase the amount of food produced at home to feed a population that could no longer depend upon imported food. Disbanded after the end of the First World War, it was re-established in 1939 and came into its own during the Second World War, reaching more than 80,000 members by 1943. It was finally wound up in 1950. There are no surviving records for the individual women in England and Wales, and although there is an alphabetical set of index cards for the 'Land Girls' of the Second World War at the Imperial War Museum, the information they contain is basic. These cards are not accessible to the public, although a photocopy of a card can be provided upon application with the full name (maiden name if unmarried at the time), date of birth and address at the time of service – contact: collections@iwm.org.uk or call the London IWM on 020 7416 5000. Alternatively, there is a complete microfiche collection of these index cards at the National Archives in the Ministry of Food collection at MAF 421. These are not available online and cannot be ordered via the catalogue; you will need to visit to search, view and take a copy of an index card, request paid research from the National Archives or commission an independent researcher to find the record for you. The guide on paying for research will explain how to do this: www.nationalarchives.gov.uk/help-with-your-research/paying-for-research. Women's Land Army veterans (or their next of kin) can apply for a commemorative badge from the Department for Environment, Food and Rural Affairs – email womenslandarmy@defra.gsi.gov.uk, visit the website, www.gov.uk/apply-womens-land-army-veterans-badge or call 01270 754160 for details of how to do this.

Other interesting websites include:

- Women at War: http://caber.open.ac.uk/schools/stanway
- Wartime Memories Project: www.wartimememoriesproject.com
- BBC People's War: www.bbc.co.uk/history/ww2peopleswar
- Royal Voluntary Service (formerly Women's Voluntary Service and WRVS): www.royalvoluntaryservice.org.uk/about-us/our-history/archive-and-heritage-collection

The information in this chapter is a brief overview of the many records and archives concerning the armed services at home and abroad. Explore these books, and others listed at the end of this book, for further information about the lives of service personnel and civilians during both wars:

Paul Reed, *Great War Lives* (Pen & Sword, 2010)
James Goulty, *Second World War Lives* (Pen & Sword, 2012)

Chapter 8

TRADES, OCCUPATIONS AND PROFESSIONS

In history, as in the modern world, people are often defined by their work. 'What do you do?' is the question most frequently asked when people meet for the first time; how they make a living is more likely to be remembered than a person's name or where they're from. An occupation is used, along with name, address, age, etc., as a way to identify someone and differentiate them from others with similar details. In the past, occupations tended to be much more long term, usually lifelong. When our ancestors were struggling to maintain food, clothing and shelter for their families, the questions of career fulfilment and work/life balance just didn't arise. Today, occupations are generally more transient and fluid – people can change careers, retrain, start businesses or take time out of the workplace (usually without the risk of starvation) much more easily than our ancestors could.

The concept of gender-specific occupations became less rigid over the course of the twentieth century. At the beginning of the 1900s gender roles were fairly fixed. If females had a job it was usually within a range of the social norms: domestic service, nursing, office work, hairdressing, etc. Until around the 1960s it was common for women to give up work when they got married and almost all did so when they had children. Similarly, males rarely strayed into 'female territory' when it came to work. Natural talent and creativity in something considered 'women's work' was not encouraged but a few men did become successful in areas such as fashion. Although occupations might be dominated by males or females, there are very few jobs today that can only be done by one or the other. We have nurses who happen to be male, but are not called 'male nurses', we have female police officers who are no longer categorised as WPCs and the suffix '-ess' has been replaced with gender-neutral job titles in many professions: head teacher or firefighter, for example.

It has always been more common than thought for people to change occupations or to have more than one way of making money, doing two or more jobs part-time. For example, I teach part-time, I run a research business and I'm a writer, but I'm also a wife and mother. Previously I worked in the library service, in retail and in the NHS. Similarly, in the past, occupations changed and adapted according to circumstances, the availability of work and the needs of the individual or family. Therefore it is not unusual for one ancestor to have a different trade, occupation or profession recorded on various documents.

Some old or obscure occupations have gradually become obsolete over the years – you won't find many hall boys, lace-makers or icemen in the late twentieth century. New professions have emerged in the fields of technology and personal growth, however, such as web designer and life coach.

Whatever work your relatives and ancestors did, there is a good chance that there is more to be discovered. Let's explore some occupations and professions of the twentieth century, what records there are and how you can find them.

Professional and Trade Associations and Directories

Whatever job your relatives did, there is a good chance that it has an association, federation, guild, society, council or institute. Some of these are statutory or regulatory bodies but others are more informal groups of people with a common interest. Professional associations can have long histories – the British Medical Association, for example, was founded 175 years ago.

Some associations have libraries or archive departments with records of former members, archives of journals, and biographies or obituaries of high-profile members. Visitors might be allowed by arrangement or there may be a research service for members of the public who want to discover information about a relative or ancestor. Access permission and costs vary with every association. So, how do you find the association of a particular trade or profession? It used to be a case of going to the nearest main library and consulting a tome called *The Directory of British Associations*, which appears to no longer be published. Now there are many websites that list professional associations ranging from acupuncture to zinc manufacturing; they include the Trade Association Forum – www.taforum.org; the British Companies website –www.britishcompanies.co.uk/organisations.htm; and a Wikipedia page –https://en.wikipedia.org/wiki/List_of_ professional _associations_in_the_United_Kingdom.

Printed directories are always a good place to start when trying to identify professions that our ancestors worked in as most professional occupations issued them regularly throughout the twentieth century. Some were simply a list of names, perhaps with addresses, but others included biographical information about education, career and retirement. Examples of popular directories include Crockford's (clergy), the Law List (lawyers) and the RIBA List (architects). Although directories are obsolete or less frequently issued today, many main county or city libraries keep runs of old trade and professional directories, although they might be held in reserve collections that will need to be ordered in advance.

Domestic Service
The TV series 'Downton Abbey' has given us an insight into a very different way of life from that we know today, but it would have been familiar to many of the relatives in our living memory. At the end of the Victorian era there were around 1.5 million

people employed as live-in domestic servants. Many average middle-class households had at least one servant, usually a maid who lived in. The upper classes, titled, new rich and landed gentry could employ as many staff as medium-sized companies of today, with a complex hierarchy including maids, cooks, footmen, butlers, drivers and valets. The largest, richest owners could have as many as sixty staff living in, with more working outside in the grounds and stables. Domestic service was the most common occupation for females at the time of the 1911 census – around 80 per cent of women who were employed worked 'in service' in some capacity, and work of this kind, although decreasing, remained a common occupation for many until the middle of the century. My aunt, before she went into nursing, started her working life in the 1930s as a between maid (or 'tweeny' as they were known) in a large country house in Dorset. She sometimes recounted the injustices of the inequality there and commented that 'the master's dogs had better food than us'.

The decline in domestic service accelerated with the First World War when women had a better choice of employment in manufacturing and public services replacing men who had been called up. A number of other factors contributed to the trade's demise: the rise in home ownership and public housing meant that staff did not need live-in work, technology such as washing machines, vacuum cleaners and refrigerators reduced the need for servants, and the levelling of social classes, particularly after the Second World War, meant that the 'master and servant' relationship went out of fashion.

Although a great many of our ancestors worked in domestic service there might not be much in the way of records except census returns showing them living in with their employers. Remember, the families that they worked for might have moved around the country, and even gone abroad, taking the staff with them. There was no central register or association for domestic workers – in fact it was not until 1938 that the National Union of

Domestic Workers was founded but the number of members, even at its peak, was less than 1,000 and the union was wound up in 1953. Records are kept in the Trades Union Congress collection, which is held by London Metropolitan University – email: tuclib@londonmet.ac.uk for information about content and access.

For servants who worked in large country or city houses, manors and halls, there is a good chance that estate records survived. Although personal information about individual servants might be sparse, browsing these records can provide a background to their work in the household and help us to understand their daily lives. In addition to records about the upkeep, maintenance and running of the household, you might find details of staff wages, employment (hiring, firing and disciplinary matters), plus general housekeeping, family events and personal letters, with possible mentions of servants by name or by title.

Estate records are sometimes kept in the private collections of the current owners but few of these properties remain intact or owned by one person, although some have been turned into hotels and educational establishments or taken over by conservation charities such as the National Trust. Household archives might not be catalogued or available to the public so you would need to apply directly to the current estate owners. In most cases, where estate records survive they will be deposited in the County (or City) Record Office in the location of the property. Remember that boundaries and local authorities sometimes changed and some record offices, archives and libraries have combined.

Low-level, unskilled domestic work was usually learned 'on the job' and any training was given by the housekeeper or other staff. Nannies might have attended a private training school such as Norland College; founded in London in 1892, it is still running but is now based in Bath: www.norland.co.uk.

Another potential source of information is domestic servants' registries. They were also known as registry offices but were similar to modern employment agencies, sometimes run as private businesses but also by charities such as the YWCA. There was usually at least one registry for domestic servants in each town and several in each city, where employers could find suitable staff and servants could find work. Where records survive, they may include, for example, interview notes, letters and references. Again, local authority record offices are the place to look for archives of registries.

My Ancestor was in Service, *A guide to sources for family historians*, published by the Society of Genealogists, offers more information about domestic servants. This book is part of the 'My Ancestor' series, which also includes titles about several other professions, including lawyers, coalminers and agricultural labourers – www.sog.org.uk/books-courses/books-publications/category/my-ancestor-series.

The following are some other popular professions of the twentieth century that have records and resources you can explore.

Merchant Seamen
The merchant navy is made up of sailors who work for commercial shipping companies and is not part of the armed services. Sailors, whether officers or crew, work on cargo ships, importing and exporting cargo around the globe. King George V awarded this trade the title 'merchant navy' in recognition of its contribution to the First World War in transporting troops and vital resources, often at considerable risk; more than 3,000 merchant vessels were sunk with great loss of life. At its peak in 1939 there were around 200,000 sailors in the merchant navy, including many from around the British Empire. During the Second World War almost 30,000 merchant seamen were killed as a result of enemy action.

If your ancestor worked in the merchant navy there is a good chance that there are surviving records that will tell you more about their working life. Key records and resources include:

Register of Merchant Seamen, 1918–1941

An original set of these Board of Trade index cards detailing just under a million merchant seamen working between the two world wars is held at Southampton City Archives (although note that it is not complete between 1918 and 1920 as many of the cards for this period were destroyed). These cards can be viewed in person at the archives, or a request can be made for a photocopy (black and white or colour) or digital photograph of the card. Charges apply. For more details see: www.southampton. gov.uk/libraries-museums/local-family-history/southampton-archives/index-merchant-seamen.aspx.

A microfiche copy of the register is available at the National Archives at Kew. However, the complete set of cards has been indexed and digital images are available on Find My Past – www.findmypast.com – under Education and Work. The content of these cards varies depending on factors such as when the seaman was employed and the length of his service. Generally, information includes:

On the front:
• Name
• Year and place of birth
• Rank or rating
• Nationality
• Discharge number
• Physical description (height, hair colour, eye colour, complexion)

On the back:
• Declaration
• Signature

- Dates and vessels
- (Cards up to 1921 may also include a photograph)

This image shows a typical card from 1920. It includes a fine photograph, some details of family members and a physical description.

A Merchant Seamen record card for William Thomas Cronan. (© *The National Archives BT350/337855; reproduced by courtesy of Ancestry.com*)

Masters and Mates Certificates (up to 1927, UK and Ireland)
These certificates were issued to sailors who qualified as masters
or mates and were also issued for service, examinations and
competency. A searchable index and digital images of original
certificates are available on Ancestry.co.uk under Immigration
and Travel, Crew lists. Content varies but certificates typically
include:

• Name
• Date and place of birth
• Address
• Port and date of issue
• Date of examination
• Service history (dates, titles, vessels)
• Certificate number

*Merchant Seamen's Campaign Medal Records, 1914–1918 and
1939–1945*
Members of the merchant navy played a vital role in both world
wars and in recognition of this many sailors were awarded
medals. You can search Discovery, the catalogue of the National
Archives, to find your merchant seaman ancestors; for more
information on the extent, content and how to view and
download these records, read: www.nationalarchives.gov.uk/
help-with-your-research/research-guides/merchant-seamen-medals-
honours.

The National Maritime Museum – www.rmg.co.uk/national-
maritime-museum – in Greenwich, London, has a vast library
containing documents, books, records and crew lists.

To discover more on this subject, read Simon Wills, *Tracing Your
Merchant Navy Ancestors* (Pen & Sword, 2012).

Medical Professions
The medical profession is made up of a number of different

occupations, including general practitioners, medical consultants, surgeons, nurses, midwives and anaesthetists.

The British Medical Association library has a complete set of the Medical Register (statutory) and the Medical Directory (commercial). Staff can sometimes undertake short searches and visits can be made by appointment. See http://bma.org.uk/ working-for-change/patient-information/your-doctor/tracing-a-historical-doctor for more information. The Royal College of General Practitioners has produced a comprehensive online guide to researching doctors working in many fields of medicine: http://www.rcgp.org.uk/about-us/history-heritage-and-archive/researching-a-medical-ancestor.aspx.

Nursing was an unregulated profession until 1919, when the Nurses Registration Act was introduced and from 1922 an annual register for England and Wales was issued by the General Nursing Council. Copies of these registers up to 1973, which are numerical, not alphabetical, are available to view at the National Archives in Kew in the DT10 and DT11 series. They are printed indexes only and digital images are not available; these records can only be searched in person. Early registers give more information; in addition to the nurse's name, they provide a home address, the name of the training hospital and date of qualification. Later registers are lists of members only. See the following guide for full details of this collection: http://discovery. nationalarchives.gov.uk/details/r/C6416.

A copy of the Roll of the Central Midwives Board 1902–1983 is also held at the National Archives in the series DV 7; again, these are not available online.

Some records for military nurses are available online. There are 15,000 records for British Army Nurses 1914–1918 in the WO 399 series at the National Archives; they are fully indexed and searchable by name. A digital image of the original record can be purchased and downloaded via the Discovery catalogue website: http://discovery.nationalarchives.gov.uk. Registers of nurses in the

Royal Navy up to 1929 can be browsed online. There are no online records specifically for the Royal Air Force but nurses who received campaign medals will be listed in the British Army medal index cards 1914–20, which are available on Ancestry.co.uk. Individual service records for military nurses can be requested from the Ministry of Defence by the nurse or next of kin only – for more information see www.gov.uk/get-copy-military-service-records.

The Royal College of Nursing has a library and heritage centre at its HQ in Cavendish Square, London, which includes a complete archive of the *British Journal of Nursing*, which is indexed and searchable; there is little in the way of biographical information on particular nurses here, however. For information on collections and access visit www.rcn.org.uk/development/library_and_heritage_services. There is a collection of some records of military nurses (Military Nurses 1856–1994) on Find My Past under Military, Armed Services and Conflict. An excellent online guide to nursing history, military and civilian nurses can be found at http://www.scarletfinders.co.uk/index.html.

Railway Workers

Before nationalisation in 1947, there was a network of privately owned railway companies operating throughout Britain. Before 1923 there were more than 100 separate companies but after that date, until 1947, there were four main companies that completed the national network: the Great Western Railway, the London & North Eastern Railway, the London, Midland & Scottish Railway and the Southern Railway. Each had its own employment records. In 1948 the railway service was nationalised and became British Rail, and there are very few records for individual employees after this date. Some staff records of railway employees have been digitised and indexed and are available online at Ancestry.co.uk under UK, Railway Employment Records, 1833–1956; these might include individual staff records or lists of employees at particular stations, apprentices and wages books. The record below is for George McKennon Johnston, who started work as a 'greaser' for the Great Western Railway at Bridgend in 1935, became a fireman by 1939 and remained employed by the company until December 1949, by which time he had moved stations several times and completed further training in 'driving turns'.

The railway employment record of George McKennon Johnston. (© *The National Archives, Railway Employment Records 1833-1956 1936-37/24876; reproduced by courtesy of Ancestry.com*)

Many more records from railway companies are held at the National Archives but these have not been indexed and are not available online. Read the guide on Railway Workers for more information: www.nationalarchives.gov.uk/help-with-your-research/research-guides/railway-workers/.

The National Railway Museum in York holds a wealth of material about British railways through the ages and the people who helped to keep them running. In addition to individual staff records, you will find much to bring your railway ancestors to life, including job descriptions, staff magazines, certificates and awards, photographs and accident reports. For more information and to plan a visit to the museum, call 08448 153139, email nrm@nrm.org.uk or visit the website: www.nrm.org.uk/NRM/ResearchAndArchive/researchhelp/FamilyHistory.

For more detailed information on researching relatives and ancestors who worked on the railways, read Di Drummond *Tracing Your Railway Ancestors* (Pen & Sword, 2010).

Police Officers
The oldest police force by far in England and Wales is the Metropolitan Police, formed by Robert Peel in 1829. Various counties established voluntary police forces over the next few decades but it wasn't until the County and Borough Police Act of 1856 that it became compulsory for a police force to be responsible for each area.

Police forces in England and Wales are autonomous and each has its own separate set of records and archives. Relatively few records of individual police officers are available online, although there are some.

The Manchester Police Index on Find My Past, transcribed by the Manchester & Lancashire Family History Society, includes records of more than 10,000 officers who served in the force up to 1941: http://search.findmypast.co.uk/search-world-records/manchester-police-index-1812-1941. The records include details such as name, age, place of birth, marital status, physical description, previous employment and religion. The original records are held in the Greater Manchester Police Museum – find out more at www.gmpmuseum.co.uk or call 0161 856 4500.

The National Archives has a number of records for the

Metropolitan Police, mostly covering the nineteenth century. Twentieth-century records that are available include police registers up to 1958, which are generally arranged by warrant number or date within the MEPO 4 set, and pension records more than fifty years old in MEPO 21; you can browse these records on Discovery, the catalogue of the National Archives: http://discovery.nationalarchives.gov.uk. There is now a Metropolitan Police Heritage Centre in West Brompton, London – www.metpolicehistory.co.uk/met-police-heritage-centre.html. It is open every weekday and entry is free. Tel. 0207 161 1234 or visit www.metpolicehistory.co.uk/met-police-heritage-centre. html for more information.

The National Archives also holds staff records of the Royal Irish Constabulary up to 1922 in the HO 184 series.

Scottish Archives Network has a useful guide to records of the police forces of Scotland at www.scan.org.uk/knowledgebase/topics/policing_topic.htm.

The British Transport Police History Group – www.btphg. org.uk – can help with information and access to staff records.

The National Police Officers Roll of Honour details more than 4,000 men and women who lost their lives in the line of duty. The following site has separate, searchable indexes for England, Wales, Scotland and Ireland: www.policememorial.org.uk/index.php?page=roll-of-honour.

There are many records from the twentieth century to be found around the country about police officers and the forces they worked in. Some are in county record offices, others in police archives or specialist collections. An internet search by county/city/borough and police archives should bring information about collections and groups within the first few results. For example, a search using the keywords Hampshire, Police and Archives results in a link to the Hampshire Constabulary History Society website: http://hampshireconstabularyhistory.org.uk. This site contains a history of the force in Hampshire and the Isle of

Wight, many photographs, personal stories, details of books and ongoing research projects. The society can help with obtaining a copy of an ancestor's personnel record up to 1926, the originals of which are held at the Hampshire Record Office. For details, email the society: hc.historysociety@gmail.com.

This National Archives research guide gives information about the police records they hold and how to access them, plus signposts to other collections: www.nationalarchives.gov.uk/help-with-your-research/research-guides/officer-in-police-force.

To find out much more about ancestors who were in the police, read Stephen Wade, *Tracing Your Police Ancestors* (Pen & Sword, 2009).

Postal Service
The Royal Mail was established in 1635 when Charles I made his postal service available to the public. By the beginning of the twentieth century it was a well-established network with uniformed workers, local post offices, cycle post routes and designated steam ships (the prefix RMS, as in RMS *Titanic*, stands for 'Royal Mail Ship', meaning that the ship had a contract to carry mail). Postal workers included female clerical workers who formed the Association of Post Office Women Clerks in 1901.

The most important collection of records relating to the postal service and its workers is the British Postal Museum and Archive in London, which is run by the Postal Heritage Trust: www.postalheritage.org.uk, tel. 020 7239 2570. The archive is open to the public every weekday with search rooms, exhibitions and staff on hand to help. Records relating to individual postal workers include those for pensions and gratuities up to 1959, and retirement records, plus records of marriage gratuities given to women when they left work to get married and death gratuities awarded to the families of postal workers who died whilst in service. These records include details of name, date of birth, rank, length of service, positions

Post Office workers in Markinch, Fife, 1913. (© *Markinch Heritage Group*)

held with dates and the amount awarded for the pension or gratuity.

The archive also holds appointment books up to 1956, which are arranged annually then alphabetically, giving details of name, date of appointment, grade and place of work. These books, including almost 1.5 million individual names, have been digitised and indexed and are available to search, view and download on Ancestry.co.uk. You can find the British Postal Service Appointment Books, 1737–1969 in the Schools, Directories & Church Histories section on Ancestry.co.uk.

Here is an image of an extract from one of the appointment books from 1951:

Date	Registered Number of Nomination Paper	Surname	Christian Name	Situation to which Nominated	Place	Minute Number	Observations
May	39299	Ashmore	Gladys B.	Tpnst.	Warwick & Leamington Spa	A29148/51	
	39849	Abbott	Frederick D.	Pman	LPR.	P3192/52	
	40340	Abbott now Abraham	Pete W.	Techn	Manr. A.	A19755/51	
	40969	Abbott	Sylvia M.	Ipnst	LTR.	A32487/51	
	41627	Arnott	Henry	Exec. Engr	Engr	A30307/38	
	41676	Armstrong	Joseph	Pman	L'pool	A26389/51	
	41647	Arnott	William	Pman	Leven Fife	A19759/51	
	44192	Armstrong	Anthony g.g.	Pman	Aldershot	A19411/51	
	44565	Allthorpe	Frederick	Pman	Kettering	A26390/51	
	45014	Allsopp	Marian R.	Ipnst	LTR.	A3111/51	
	45359	Athon	Edwin	Techn G s	Sheffield TA	h3048/51	
	45606	Armstrong	Goram	P. to	Coventry	A35204/50	
	46285/39	Aago	Aanya.	P. to	Enfield.	A12648/40	
June	48348	Ambrose	Ernest g.	Ito mech.	Factories	A26391/51	
	48349	Ashton	Valerie	Ipnst	Derby.	A26392/51	

Extract from a postal workers' appointment book. (© *British Postal Museum and Archive*)

Publicans

Pub landlords traditionally owned or rented an inn, tavern or public house and were granted a licence, issued by the local courts, to sell alcohol. Breweries owned many pubs in the twentieth century and 'tied' the landlords to selling only their beer. Eventually, by the 1980s around 90 per cent of pubs had become tied to a brewery, and the remainder, instead of displaying a brewery's name, would proudly declare that they were a 'Free House'.

There are no central records for pubs and landlords but there are a number of places to look. The records of the National Licensed Victuallers Association up to 1992 have been deposited at the London Metropolitan Archives, reference number GB 0074 ACC/3122. These records contain papers, minutes of meetings, records of events such as banquets and dinners, annual reports and copies of badges and banners. If your relative was involved in this association it is worth searching this collection, which is available for public inspection. However, some personal information may have restricted access. Contact the LMA for further information: email ask.lma@cityoflondon.gov.uk or telephone 020 7332 3820. Archives for the Quarter Sessions (courts that granted licences) are usually deposited at county and city record offices, although they are often not indexed and there may be date access restrictions.

There are some records of licensed victuallers online but only for the very early part of the century. Surrey Licensed Victuallers Registers up to 1903 are available to search and view online on Ancestry.co.uk.

Street directories and photograph collections in local libraries and record offices are a good source of information about the pubs in their area. You can track changes of name and landlord and find pictures of pubs through the decades. If you want a photograph or postcard of a pub from the time that your relatives owned or managed it, try the Images tab of any popular search engine. Picture postcards of buildings were very popular in the early and mid-century and many survive. Some are sold by private collectors and others have been scanned and uploaded by pub history enthusiasts or local history associations. The Pub History Society has a useful website containing much information, including how to research particular pubs: www.pub historysociety.co.uk.

There are also some societies or associations for brewing and pubs in particular counties and regions, such as www. gloucestershirepubs.co.uk and www.midlandspubs.co.uk. The people involved with this type of society tend to be very knowledgeable and willing to help with memories and photographs. Jeremy Gibson's *Victuallers' Licences* (Family History Partnership, 2009, third edition) is a helpful guide. It is currently out of print but there are copies in circulation, both new and second-hand.

Company Directors

Directors are responsible for running a company and every limited company must have at least one director. They are not necessarily owners but have legal responsibilities and, because they are accountable, their details – name, date of birth and home address – are public information. If a director was also the sole or majority shareholder, there might be additional information about him or her in the company records, including documents about the formation of the company in the original handwriting of the person who composed and submitted the records.

Records of companies still trading, including details of the directors, are held by Companies House in Cardiff: www.gov.uk/government/organisations/companies-house, tel. 0303 123 4500, email enquiries@companies-house.gov.uk. There is a £20 charge for an archive search on a company. Some records can also be viewed and ordered online. Details of current and recently resigned (within around the last twenty years) company directors can be obtained online for the nominal fee of £1 but currently you will need the company name or number to obtain these from the Companies House search site: https://beta.companieshouse.gov.uk.

Directors can be searched online by name at various commercial sites. These offer limited information for free, including names of the companies that a director works (or has worked) for: https://companycheck.co.uk and http://directors.findthecompany.co.uk are two popular sites, or you can just type the name of your relatives and 'company director' into any search engine for public information including date of birth and companies that the director worked for.

There is also a register of disqualified directors from 1986 that is fully searchable: http://wck2.companieshouse.gov.uk//dirsec.

Records of dissolved companies (companies that are no longer trading) are of most interest to researchers, but they are not comprehensive. Also, older records are filed by company number, not by name, and there are no indexes by name of director beyond 1937. Records for recently dissolved companies (within the last twenty years) are held at Companies House. Some, but not all, records before this have been transferred to Board of Trade records at the National Archives and are held in the series BT 31, BT 34 and BT41, which are searchable on the Discovery catalogue by company name or number.

Companies also have their own records and when they cease trading these records might be destroyed, kept by any company that succeeded the original one or transferred to a public repository such as a local record office. However, if a company went into liquidation, then the records held by the company itself became the property of the official receiver.

For more detailed information about company records read the comprehensive National Archives research guide: www.nationalarchives.gov.uk/help-with-your-research/research-guides/companies-and-businesses-further-research. John Orbell, *A Guide to Tracing the History of a Business* (Phillimore & Co. Ltd, 2009) also has comprehensive information on historical business and company records.

Other Online Records

As the great digitisation projects continue, trade and professional directories and employment records are becoming more widely available. Usually these start with the oldest records and work forwards, but some for at least the first half of the twentieth century have been released as part of an ongoing drive to make these records accessible. Here are some of the collections that can be accessed at present via Ancestry and Find My Past, but it is worth checking back on both sites for release dates of later records.

On Ancestry:
• Medical Registers – 1959

- Mechanical Engineer Records – 1930
- Civil Engineer List – 1930
- Electrical Engineer Lists – 1930
- Crockford's Clerical Directories – 1932
- Royal Aero Club Aviators' Certificates 1910–1950

On Find My Past:
- Trade Union Membership Registers (various dates, some up to 1945)
- Royal Household Staff – 1924
- Teachers Registration Council Registers 1914–1948
- Dental Surgeons Directory (1925 only)
- Companies House Directors 2002–2014

Chapter 9

LAND, PROPERTY AND PLACES

Landowners

As we explored in the section on domestic service, the decline of the landed gentry took place over the first few decades of the twentieth century. However, the titled and industry rich still held much British land in the form of estates, some of which had been in families for generations, even centuries. *Burke's Landed Gentry*, a volume first published in three volumes in the 1830s, listed 'Commoners of Great Britain and Ireland, enjoying Territorial Possessions or High Official Rank, but uninvested with Heritable Honours'. Although published as three volumes (listed alphabetically by name of family) well into the twentieth century, it was subsequently reduced to one volume and editions were issued less frequently. The criteria for inclusion changed too; whereas once only owners of 500 acres or more were included, this criterion was reduced to 200 acres by the end of the century. Families whose ancestors held estates and were included in previous editions might also feature, even where the land is no longer in their ownership. Most libraries have at least one copy of *Burke's Landed Gentry*, even if it is an older edition. Records of landowners and their tenants can often be found in estate papers; see the section on domestic service for more information.

Property Records

Researching the properties in which our relatives and ancestors lived can add another dimension to our perception of how they lived. If we can place them in a house, street, town or village at a certain time we can imagine them there, going about their daily lives. Walking down the same road, or sitting in the same rooms, as our ancestors can bring a thrill of connection that cannot be experienced just by looking at records. Maps and pictures of places where our kin once lived give substance to research that is often just about people. Following up addresses on certificates, census returns or in directories and registers, it is usually possible to locate online both contemporary and modern maps. Large-scale maps showing individual properties are held at county libraries and, although permission to copy them varies between authorities, it is usually possible to take a digital image by camera or scanner, which can be cropped, manipulated and printed to add to your research files or framed to hang on a wall. The British Library also has a comprehensive collection of local Ordnance Survey maps, although some are on microfiche – this guide explains the collection and has links to other sources for maps: www.bl.uk/collection-guides/ordnance-survey-mapping.

The Valuation Office Survey was undertaken by statute throughout England and Wales between 1910 and 1915. Many (but not all) of the 95,000 Field Books survive in the National Archives, but they are not indexed by property and are not available online. These books describe the use and value of houses, farms, properties, land and buildings and also include the names of residents and owners. There is a detailed guide to this collection, including information on how to identify the records that cover a particular area: www.nationalarchives.gov.uk/help-with-your-research/research-guides/valuation-office-survey-land-value-ownership-1910-1915.

The deeds (ownership papers) of a property can help you to trace previous owners and provide a description of the property. Modern deeds are usually held either by the owner, by a mortgage company or by a solicitor. The deeds to your own property might include information about every previous owner, although the law now only requires that ownership within the last thirty years is recorded. Older title deeds may have been deposited by solicitors in record offices and libraries. The current title registers (owners) and title plans (showing position and boundary maps) for properties in England and Wales, which may include the history of owners, boundary changes, division of land and previous sales, can be purchased from the Land Registry; apply online at www.landregistry.gov.uk or call 0300 006 0411. There are also fourteen Land Registry offices throughout England and Wales, although you may need to make an appointment. For their locations see: www.gov.uk/government/publications/land-registry-office-addresses/office-addresses.

Locations

You can widen the perspective to look at not just the properties your relatives inhabited but the locations in which they lived. The churches and schools they attended, the village greens where they may once have sat, the streets they walked along, the land they worked on – viewing these on maps and in photographs, reading descriptions or even visiting in person can bring our ancestors to life in an environment that would have been so familiar to them. You can get to know locations, even those many miles away, without leaving your armchair. Every local authority, at least at present, has a library service. Staff are usually happy to recommend books about an area that you are interested in and using the terms (place) and library will usually bring a top result, or at least the correct link on the first page; for example, typing in 'Romsey' (a former home town of mine in Hampshire) and 'library' instantly brings up the library's address, phone number, website and even a photograph of the building.

Google maps – www.google.co.uk/maps – is a twenty-first-century revelation, although some people feel it represents an invasion of privacy. A fleet of vans with mounted cameras have driven around the streets, roads and lanes of the UK (and indeed many of the countries in the western world) taking images in order to make it possible for anyone to make a virtual trip to almost anywhere in the country. I have just spent a nostalgic half-hour wandering the village where I grew up, viewing the house I once lived in, the little school that I attended, the village green where I played and the lanes that I cycled along as a child. The images may not be completely up to date (these pictures were taken four years ago) but they can give a sense of a place. If you want to see the places where your relatives were born, lived and died, this is a great way to 'visit' without travelling. Taking virtual visits a step further is the introduction of webcams – cameras recording live images, day and night, for global transmission. Many famous landmarks, city scenes, beaches, beauty spots and remote hideaways have webcams that can instantly transport you to places that may be far away or closer to home. You can use a webcam portal such as www.earthcam.com or simply type the name of a place and 'webcam' into a search engine to see if there is one operating in a place where your family has a connection.

One of the most widely used websites for locating people in places is Curious Fox: www.curiousfox.com. A brilliant idea, simply executed, it is a forum site based around locations, rather than names or families. It is described as 'the village by village contact site for anyone researching family history, genealogy and local history in the UK and Ireland', although searches can also be made by town or county. It is free to join and to post queries but there is a nominal annual membership fee (currently £5.50) to contact others. This site can be used to locate ancestors or living relatives, exchange memories or request information. Typically, an entry posted by a member might ask if anyone has any information about the X family who lived in the village of Y around 1922. This is a great way to connect with people who have a wealth of local knowledge.

Another medium connecting people with links to particular locations is the Facebook Group facility. Special interest groups, either closed or public, can be formed by anyone. Invitations to join a group can be issued by the founder and members or people can ask to join. Romsey Revisited is a closed group with more than 3,200 members, all with a connection to the Hampshire town. Photographs and memories are shared, questions asked and members reunited with family and friends.

There are numerous family history societies around the country. They are usually formed by, and mostly made up of, members with local ancestors and family connections, rather than people just doing their family history. As such, societies can have members from all over the world who happen to have ancestors in the location that the society covers. Often these are county societies but a number of counties also have several district societies. Membership fees are usually nominal (less than £20 per year), which typically includes a quarterly magazine, access to any records or indexes the society holds, regular meetings and talks, advice and a free or subsidised 'look-up' service of local records by volunteer members. Most societies have either online forums where members can post queries and exchange information or magazine pages dedicated to appeals for information about families and ancestors. Considering the charges that family history enthusiasts regularly pay for certificates, subscriptions to online services, for photocopies, postage and transport, etc., a small annual fee to join a society can be well worth the expense. The Federation of Family History Societies has a comprehensive A–Z list of societies in England, Wales and Ireland on its website – www.ffhs.org.uk – or simply enter the name of the county and 'family history society' into a search engine.

Local history associations are another way to connect with places where your relatives lived. Associated with counties, cities, towns, villages and suburbs, these are often well established groups, formally run by a committee. The remit of history groups varies but typically they might collect local artefacts, books and historical documents, petition for the preservation of local buildings, hold exhibitions, undertake research projects and publish books and papers. For example, Bitterne Local History Society near Southampton was formed in 1981 when the construction of a dual carriageway meant much of the old centre was demolished and replaced with a shopping precinct. Bitterne is a settlement that originated in the eleventh century, growing up around a manor house, which became first a village and then a city suburb. The society campaigns for the preservation and protection of important buildings and features, rescues and restores artefacts, organises talks, trips and local walks, publishes a range of material and has a building that operates as a bookshop, charity shop, museum and place to research – see www.bitterne.net.

If your family has strong links with a particular place, a local history society can be a good way to explore the area they inhabited in greater depth. Getting involved with, or volunteering for, a local history group is also a way to give back to the area that shaped and supported your ancestors. Local History Online – www.local-history.co.uk – lists many of the local history groups in England and Wales, plus some in Scotland and Ireland.

School Records

At the turn of the century poor law schools were becoming less common and most elementary schools were run either by school boards or by the local church. Education was compulsory up to the age of 13. In 1902 a new Education Act was introduced, which transferred responsibility for education into the hands of local authorities. In 1918 a new Act (not implemented until 1921) raised the leaving age to 14 and made attendance compulsory. The upper age of compulsory education was changed to 15 in 1947 and to 16 in 1973.

Although there are many school records available covering the first part of the century, most of them are concerned with finance, buildings, attendance figures and performance; they do not necessarily include any information about individual pupils.

119

Surviving documents such as registers, reports, meeting notes and diaries may be subject to a closure period of between fifty and a hundred years. The schools that your ancestors attended, if still in existence, may keep their own archives but it is more likely that they were deposited in local authority archives after a period of time. My own Church of England village school claims to have 'no idea' where its records from the 1970s are, or if they were even kept. There is a comprehensive set of records, however, in the county record office, covering the period up to 1942. The documents include 'lists of pupils, lists of attendances, distribution of prizes, medical inspection reports and after care, with correspondence'. There are some records online, usually in the form of admission registers, with varying amounts of detail: some are simply a list of names, others have dates and may be annotated.

Find My Past has National School Admission Registers and Log-Books up to 1914. Some of these records are rich in detail and can include information such as:

• Surname and first name
• Date (or year) of birth
• Name and location of school
• Dates of admission and leaving
• Names of a child's parents
• Father's occupation
• Exam results
• Absences and illness
• Planned destination after school

Although it is not yet a comprehensive collection, there are currently records of around 4 million children, although many of these are from before 1900. This is an ongoing project, however, with records being continuously added.

There is also a category called Britain, School and University

Register Books 1264–1930, which has a selection of detailed records from a few schools throughout the country, although many of these are from before the twentieth century. Other categories for education include British Army Schoolchildren (to 1932), Glamorgan Schools Admission Registers and Manchester School Admissions Registers.

All of the above can be found at www.findmypast.co.uk under Search, Education and Work, then Schools and Education.

Ancestry has a handful of registers under School Lists & Yearbooks, although some of these are not indexed by the child's name and can only be browsed by year. You will need to select United Kingdom in the 'Filter by location' box to eliminate most of the records, which cover the USA. The UK records that extend into the twentieth century include:

- London, England, School Admissions and Discharges –1911
- West Yorkshire, England, Reformatory School Records –1914
- London School Registers (currently only two parishes to around 1990; original records are at the London Metropolitan Archives)

Some school records can record details of national and local events that affected the children's attendance and well-being. Northam School in Southampton, for example, had a large number of children whose fathers, brothers and uncles were dockworkers and merchant seamen. More than a hundred children from the school lost at least one relative when the *Titanic* sank in 1912. The entry in the school diary for 15 April 1912, written by the headmistress, records: 'A great many girls are absent owing to the sad news regarding the "Titanic". Fathers and brothers are on the vessel & some of the little ones have been in tears all afternoon.' The entry two days later reads: 'I feel I must record the sad aspect in school today owing to the "Titanic" disaster. So many of the crew belong to Northam & it is pathetic to watch the children's grief.'

These records and more can be seen at Southampton's 'Titanic Story', a permanent exhibition at Sea City Museum, Southampton: http://seacitymuseum.co.uk.

There is a large History of Education collection including documents, textbooks, manuals and children's exercise books from the seventeenth century onwards at the Museum of the History of Science, Technology and Medicine in Leeds: http://arts.leeds.ac.uk/museum-of-hstm.

University Records

If one of your relatives attended a university there is a good chance that records of their time there have survived and can be accessed. The older the records, the more likely it is that they will be open. University libraries usually welcome members of the public to visit for research or study, although you may need to apply for a day ticket and produce identification. Copies of research papers and dissertations by former students may have been retained and catalogued. Alumni departments record details of former students and aim to maintain the connection between them, the university and fellow students. Events such as exhibitions, fundraising efforts and landmark celebrations (e.g. centenaries) are arranged with the help of the alumni office and aim to continually involve former students. Lists of living former students may be subject to Data Protection, although the university may be prepared to issue confirmation of dates attended and perhaps the degree that was studied. Searching online by the name of the university and the place will almost always find the correct website immediately, although do remember that some locations have more than one university since many former polytechnics were upgraded to university status. There are very few alumni records available online for the twentieth century and it is best initially to make enquiries to the university concerned to see what records are held. The portal site Archives Hub – http://archiveshub.ac.uk – enables you to search descriptions of archives held at over 250 institutions across the UK.

Chapter 10

MIGRATION AND TRAVEL

Migration has been a part of Britain's story for centuries. From the Norman, Roman and Viking invasions to the colonisation of the British Empire, there has been population movement. People left and people came, sometimes to rule, often to work, but usually with the hope of a better life. The twentieth century saw increasing migration from and to Britain with the growth of commerce and industry, more efficient transport and changes in the political landscape.

Travelling abroad for pleasure was a rare thing before the twentieth century, a pastime that could only be afforded by the very rich. British settlement in the colonies meant that, increasingly, British subjects could travel to numerous destinations around the globe yet still feel at home. My own paternal great-grandmother, Lilian, had a taste for adventure and travelled to Rhodesia (now Zimbabwe) several times between the 1930s and the 1950s, living there for long periods with her third 'husband' (but that's another story!). Although she returned to Britain eventually and ended her days in a flat in Bournemouth, she apparently often longed to go back to her 'second home'.

Between 1890 and 1914 an estimated 125,000 people emigrated to the USA every year, with 50,000 per year going to live in Canada and 25,000 per year to Australia. Emigration to Australia was particularly encouraged with the passing of the Empire Settlement Act of 1922, in which the Australian and British governments cooperated to encourage emigration with

Australian government poster, 1928. (© *National Archives of Australia*)

the help of subsidised fares, training, living allowances, grants, jobs and land for farming.

Some, however, left Britain not by choice but as a result of policies that today seem misguided at best. The practice of 'child migration' began in the nineteenth century but continued well into the twentieth century. Orphaned, pauper and illegitimate children, often seen as a burden on society in their home parishes, were sent abroad permanently through a government scheme that was facilitated by local authorities and children's charities. These children, usually between the ages of 7 and 10 but some as young as 3, were seen as 'good stock', not only to work in the colonies but also to boost the white British population and ensure 'racial unity'. At the policy's peak in the post-war era thousands of children were shipped to Australia, New Zealand, Canada and Rhodesia, with the cooperation of these countries' governments. Very few of these children ever returned to Britain.

The two world wars brought about the immigration of hundreds of thousands of working men and their families from across the empire. Some 1.3 million Indian soldiers had fought for the British in the First World War and some of these, together with around 60,000 merchant seamen from India, came to Britain between and after the wars. After the Second World War a desperate shortage of home-grown labour led to an active recruitment campaign for working men from further afield. Around 160,000 Eastern Europeans and Italians settled in the UK in the late 1940s as the abundance of work promised prosperity that they no longer had in their homelands. With the empire fast disappearing, and the continuing shortfall of workers, Britain turned to the West Indies as a source of labour and to boost numbers in the armed services. Several hundred West Indian men arrived on the *Empire Windrush* in 1948, the first of thousands who continued to arrive with the promise of work in their former 'mother country'.

At the same time Australia was selling the dream of a new life in a land of sunshine. The Assisted Passage Migration Scheme, also known as the 'Ten Pound Pom' drive, offering one-way travel for a token £10, tempted almost 1.5 million Brits who were keen to leave behind the cold climate and continued rationing. Although 250,000 did not stay for more than the compulsory two years, well over a million British settlers remained there permanently.

Political upheaval and unrest in the East African countries of Kenya, Tanzania and Uganda in the 1960s and 1970s meant that displaced Asian citizens of these former colonies were granted permission to settle in Britain. Between 1960 and 1972 around 45,000 East African Asians, including 27,000 who had been forced to leave Uganda by Idi Amin's government, came to live in Britain.

Due to subsequent legislation that sought to restrict immigration, it became more difficult to come to the UK permanently without strong family connections, a specialist skill or a profession in which employees were needed. However, the relaxing of European Union residential and working restrictions has meant that in recent decades the movement of citizens within Europe has become easier.

A Family Story

Let's look at a typical story of immigration to the UK, but one that is very personal to me. My husband's parents were born on different continents but both had the same heritage. My father-in-law was from the Punjab, the son of a village herbalist and one of twelve children. In keeping with tradition his marriage was arranged and his bride's family had connections with someone in the same village. My mother-in-law was a trainee teacher, born and raised in Kenya, the daughter of a police superintendent. She did not meet her husband before they married in 1953. The early years of the marriage were blessed; although married in India, they lived in various locations in Kenya, where Dad worked as a hospital administrator. They lived in government houses and had cooks, drivers, nannies and gardeners. Mum held coffee mornings and garden parties, sewed and knitted and helped the children with homework. Their three children went to private schools and the family travelled by ship every two years to visit paternal

---

relatives in India. They must have thought that this way of life would go on for ever.

As is often the case, politics influenced the lives of ordinary people. Jomo Kenyatta became the prime minister of Kenya following independence from Britain in 1963 and was appointed president of the newly formed Republic of Kenya in 1964. One of the major policies of his government was 'Kenyanisation'; he wanted to return all public employment to native Kenyans and gradually, over a number of years, former immigrants to the British colony were removed from their posts. This meant that my Indian father-in-law eventually lost his job, although he remained in post for several years to help train the Kenyans who would run public services. The redundancy package was generous, however, and included passage for the whole family to any destination in the world. As British passport holders, by virtue of Mum's birth in the colony and with a few relatives already in the England, the decision was not difficult. My in-laws felt that England held the best prospects for their children in terms of education and employment. The children had learned English in school and watched British TV programmes like 'The Saint' and 'The Avengers'; their parents read English novels and newspapers. Although sad to leave Kenya, they were excited at the prospect of a new life in a land that they thought would be familiar.

Reality dawned on a wet, November day in 1971 when they landed at Heathrow. Driving along the grey streets they were shocked to see tiny houses and litter on the pavements. Lodging in two rooms while Dad looked for permanent work, that first winter, cold and dark, was a desperately depressing time for them all. Learning to use buses and get used to the currency, my (future) husband went to college, wearing an overcoat and gloves for the first time, while his younger siblings started school. His father soon found work as an education welfare officer and his mother started a part-time clerical job

and they bought a house the following year. The rest is history
. . . my husband went to university, got a job in the library
service, moved to Southampton, we met and married and now
have two adult children – all because of events that happened
decades ago, half a world away.

COLONY AND PROTECTORATE OF KENYA

BRITISH NATIONALITY ACT, 1948, SECTION 6 (1)

APPLICATION FOR REGISTRATION AS A CITIZEN OF THE UNITED
KINGDOM AND COLONIES UNDER SECTION 6 (1) OF THE ACT, MADE
BY AN ADULT BRITISH SUBJECT OR CITIZEN OF EIRE, ON THE
GROUND OF ORDINARY RESIDENCE IN THE COLONY AND PROTEC-
TORATE OF KENYA OR ON THE GROUND OF CROWN SERVICE UNDER HER
MAJESTY'S GOVERNMENT.

[*The instructions for completing this form should be read carefully before the form is
filled up. Portions of the form which are not applicable must be struck out and initialed in
every case.*]

The heading of a UK Citizenship application, Government of Kenya,
1968.

Records of Twentieth-century Migration and Travel
Passenger Lists
Passenger lists from ships that travelled between countries and
continents can be a great resource for family research, whether
your ancestor travelled abroad or visited Britain for work or
pleasure, whether they arrived here to live or emigrated to another
country. Passenger lists were maintained by the Board of Trade and
for years they were held in the National Archives, but the name
of the ship, the destination or port of departure and the date were
needed to locate records of individuals who travelled. A massive
indexing and digitisation programme in the 1990s means that
these records are now searchable by name and viewable online,
and digital images of the original documents can be downloaded.

Outgoing and incoming passenger lists cover only journeys
between the UK and ports outside Europe and the
Mediterranean; sailings between destinations in Europe,

including those between mainland Britain and Irish ports, are not included. However, many ships stopped for passengers to board or disembark en route to ports further afield; for example, passenger liners to the USA might leave Ireland then dock in England, France and Spain before heading off across the Atlantic.

The information contained in outgoing passenger lists varies between dates, routes and shipping lines. Some are typed, some are handwritten, some are on pre-printed forms, some include ages, addresses and occupations and others just names. Searches can be narrowed by gender, age, name of ship, port of departure and destination. Results are displayed giving the name, approximate age, year, port of departure and destination. From the 1930s entries included the abbreviation 'T' if an incoming passenger was a tourist on a short-term visit.

UK Outward Passenger Lists, 1890–1960 are available on FindMyPast.co.uk and Ancestry.co.uk. Ancestry also has UK Incoming Passenger Lists, 1878–1960.

A South American Connection

Mark knew little about his paternal grandfather's origins. Reg, who was born at the end of the 1800s and died in the 1960s, when Mark was a child, lived a quiet life in Southampton with his family. Mark's dad had a vague idea that his father was born abroad or at sea but knew nothing more. The first clue came when the 1911 census of England and Wales recorded Reginald's place of birth as Argentina. As the family (mother and siblings but no father) was living in Southampton at the time, a search was made for a record of their journey back to England. Reginald, his mother and siblings were found on the passenger list of second-class British subjects aboard the steam ship *Amazon*, a Royal Mail Steam Packet Company vessel that sailed from Buenos Aires to Southampton in March 1907.

To discover the name of Reg's father, the birth certificate of his younger sister was obtained. This revealed that his name was Samuel Fermage Osborne, an electrician in the Argentine Navy. Reg, his mother and siblings remained in England but Samuel continued to travel to and from Argentina to work and visit his family until the early 1930s; all of these journeys were recorded on various passenger lists. He returned to England for the last time in September 1931 aboard the SS *Astaris*, arriving in Southampton on 25 September; he was 66. He stayed until the following June, then left on his final journey, this time from Cardiff on the SS *Zapala*. He never returned to England and his wife died a widow in 1939. So far a record of Samuel's death has not been found.

Extract from passenger list, SS *Zapala*, Cardiff to Buenos Aires, 1932. (© *The National Archives BT27/147656; reproduced by courtesy of Ancestry.com*)

Naturalisation and Citizenship Records

Records of this nature are only available online for around the first decade or so of the twentieth century.

Naturalisation Certificates and Declarations of British Nationality were maintained by the Home Office. Digital images are available on Ancestry.co.uk up to 1912 only. The format for each entry is two pages of a pre-printed book giving particulars of the person concerned, his family and his origins. Citizens were required to sign an 'Oath of Allegiance' to the reigning sovereign of their new country.

Copies of duplicate naturalisation certificates up to 1982 and naturalisation case papers up to 1934 are held at the National Archives at Kew: www.nationalarchives.gov.uk. There are no specific indexes to these records by name as they can be held within various collections, but entries relating to papers held can be searched for on Discovery, the National Archives catalogue. This guide gives a more detailed explanation: www.national archives.gov.uk/help-with-your-research/research-guides/ naturalised-britons.

For certificates of British citizenship from 1949 to 1986 you will need to apply for a search to see if a copy of a naturalisation certificate is held (this initial search is free). If an entry is found you can purchase a photocopy of the certificate for a nominal fee, or a certified copy for a charge, currently around £26.

The following National Archives research guide gives more detailed information:

www.nationalarchives.gov.uk/help-with-your-research/
research-guides/naturalisation-british-citizenship.

Archives in Other Countries and Colonial Records

As we have seen, British people travelled, settled, worked and ruled in countries all over the world. It follows, therefore, that records relating to, and based in, those countries can contain valuable information about relatives and ancestors who visited or lived there. In the case study above relating to Samuel Osborne and his family in Argentina, for example, in addition to family records found here, researchers uncovered much information about the lives of Samuel and his family in Buenos Aires. He appeared on a national census there and the birth of his son was registered in Buenos Aires (in Spanish but recording much detail about his family). There may also be records relating to his long-term employment with the Argentine Navy. All of this builds a fascinating picture of his life there that is rich with detail and brings it to life.

Most countries have a national archive of some description and in every country there are genealogists and researchers who know the local records and can locate and supply information about your relatives and copies of relevant documents. A good starting point is to find out about records, resources and availability in the country where your relative lived. You can do this simply by entering the terms 'Argentina' and 'Archives', for example, into a search engine. The first page of results brings up information about, and a link to, the General Archive of the Nation, Argentina, in Buenos Aires.

Records of births, marriages and deaths of British subjects were usually (but not always) recorded by British official offices in the country in question. Records were then gathered, collated and the information sent back to Britain for indexing.

Certificates of these overseas events can be issued by the General Register Office for England and Wales. Indexes can be searched online in the British Nationals born/married/died overseas record sets at www.findmypast.co.uk and certificates for overseas events can be ordered from the General Register Office: www.gro.gov.uk. The General Register Office: Miscellaneous Foreign Returns collection (up to 1969) and General Register Office: Foreign Registers and Returns (up to 1960) can be found at the National Archives (at RG32 and RG33 respectively).

For more information, read the following research guide on the National Archives website: www.nationalarchives.gov.uk

/help-with-your-research/research-guides/birth-marriage-death-sea-or-abroad.

A helpful book on this subject is Geoffrey Yeo's *The British Overseas: A Guide to Records of Their Births, Baptisms, Marriages, Deaths and Burials, Available in the United Kingdom* (Guildhall Library Research Guides, 1995).

A great site to explore for records worldwide is Cyndi's List of Genealogy Sites on the Internet: www.cyndislist.com. This well-established, extensive resource is invaluable for family research with over 300,000 links and information about resources for family history in almost every country.

FamilySearch – https://familysearch.org/search – states on its website that it has the largest collection of genealogical and historical records in the world, totalling more than 4 billion individual names worldwide.

For copies of official documents in other countries it is worth contacting the British Embassy or Consulate in that country for information on procedures and costs. Visit www.gov.uk/government/world/organisations for information about, and links to, offices worldwide.

If you are new to family history, don't have time to undertake research yourself or find the range of resources confusing, it may be worth investing in a specialist researcher for the countries that your relatives visited or lived in. They do not necessarily need to be based in that country, just have a knowledge of the records and how to access them. To find an accredited, established or registered researcher, there are professional associations with websites that can be searched by research speciality or location – try: www.agra.org.uk (Britain), www.sag.org.au (Australia) or www.apgen.org (USA and worldwide).

Joining a family history society is a great way to discover more about where your ancestors lived, as well as enabling you to exchange information and establish connections. Societies exist in numerous locations around the world but some that are closer to home can also help with a wealth of knowledge and access to records about your relatives. Families in British India Society (FIBIS) is one such organisation. It is 'a self-help organisation devoted to members researching their ancestors and the background against which they led their lives in India under British rule'. Visit www.fibis.org for more information and to join. For contact details and links to family history societies in Australia, Canada, USA and New Zealand, visit the website of the Federation of Family History Societies and click on the 'Overseas' tab, or call 01455 203133.

You can find information on ancestors in service in colonial India, including the areas that are now Pakistan, Bangladesh and Burma, on Find My Past in the India Office List, 1933 (under Education and Work).

Chapter 11

TRACING LIVING RELATIVES

As explored in the Introduction, keeping in touch with, and rediscovering, living relatives can not only enhance our family research but also strengthen family ties. Whether you want to locate relatives with whom you have lost touch, or identify living descendants of a common ancestor, there are a number of methods and sources. These days it should be possible for you to find relatives using your computer without needing to leave your chair, although there may be a few expenses and it might take a little time.

The following list contains a few of the websites and organisations that you can use to locate relatives. As mentioned in the sections on electoral registers and telephone directories in Chapter 4, there are a few commercial websites that you can use to locate relatives on current and recent registers, and also phone listings:

• **www.peopletracer.co.uk** – the electoral register from 2002, searchable by name and location. You must register to use this site and purchase credits to search and view results. Packages start at £7.95 for six credits.

• **www.192.com** – combines the public electoral register from 2002, telephone listings and company director information. Although some searches and results, such as telephone directory entries, are free, you will need to register and purchase credits (minimum charge currently £9.95 + VAT for six credits) to view full entries in other categories.

- **www.findmypast.com** – as described in previous sections, this site offers UK electoral registers, 2002–2014, under Census, Land and Surveys in world records. You will need to purchase credits or subscribe to view the results of any searches.
- **www.thephonebook.bt.com** – also previously mentioned, this online searchable phone directory is free to use, unlike most of the commercial directory enquiry services that you can call.

There are also sites where you can search for relatives or link with others who share your ancestry:

- **www.genesreunited.co.uk** – this site offers a way to link with others who are researching the same ancestors as you. It's free to register, and you can search by name, input your family tree information and find out if there are others registered who have the same connections. There are costs for subscription or credits (minimum £4.95) to send messages and search other records on the site.
- **www.myheritage.com** – a global site combining individual family trees with historical records. It's free to register for a basic site and input details of up to 250 family members but there are cost packages to access additional facilities.
- **www.one-name.org.uk** – If your surname, or the surname of the relatives you are seeking, is uncommon, it can be worth contacting someone who is researching the surname and has a knowledge of its history and distribution, via the Guild of One Name Studies website.
- **www.cousinconnect.com** – described as 'the Genealogy Query Database', this is a message-board site designed purely for posting queries and connecting relatives. It is completely free to use, although you will need to register using your email address.
- **www.missing-you.net** - this is a message-board site where you can post appeals for information about relatives, whether you

have lost touch or never met. You can search by name, county, town or region. It is free to use but you will need to log in using an email address.

If online searching is not successful, the **Salvation Army** runs a subsidised Family Tracing Service to reunite close relatives, however long ago contact was lost. Visit www.salvation army.org.uk/reuniting-families to find out more, email family. tracing@salvationarmy.org.uk or call 0845 634 4747. Note that the Salvation Army does not undertake adoption research, look for anyone under 18 or conduct searches for 'possible' relatives (e.g. alleged fathers).

Tracing Forward to Find Living Descendants

Descendant searching – tracing a family line forward in time to identify and locate living descendants of common ancestors – is becoming more popular as online indexes of births, marriages and deaths have made this type of search easier to conduct.

Case Study

This is an example using entries from the General Register Office indexes of births, marriages and deaths to show how events in indexes can be linked together to trace descendants of a common ancestor. (Some details have been changed.)

Initial information provided was that a woman whose maiden name was Mavis Winston had died and her relatives needed to be traced. Her death certificate recorded that she was born in Kelston, Somerset, on 22 February 1916. Her only known relative, her sister-in-law, remembered that Mavis's parents were called Ada and Sid. She thought that Sid had died in Bristol in the 1950s, and had a brother called Fred, who was married to a woman called Hettie. She was sure that they had two children, a boy and a girl, and that the boy was called Donny.

A search for her birth record in Somerset in the first quarter of 1916 found one likely candidate: *Mavis Winston, mother's maiden name Price, district of Kelston.* An index search for the marriage of her parents confirms that this is the correct entry: *Second quarter 1915, Ada C.E. Price to Sidney G. Winston, district of Kelston.*

Note how the mother's maiden name on Mavis's birth entry matches the marriage entry for her parents. With marriages there will be two entries, one under the name of the bride and the other under the name of the groom.

A search for the index entry of Sidney's death locates the following: *Sidney George Winston, age 68, died first quarter 1958, district of Bristol.* This suggested that Sidney was born around 1890; a search for his birth from about 1888 to 1892 found the following entry: *Sidney George Winston, born last quarter 1889, district of Bedminster.* (Bedminster is on the border of Somerset and Gloucestershire. In 1896 the district was incorporated into South Bristol.)

Note that at this stage, tracing forward hasn't started. This is because it is usually necessary to 'go back to come forward' – in other words, it is important to confirm information about the previous generation to ensure that you are following the correct line.

Moving on to Sidney's brother, Fred, a search was made ten years either side of Sidney's birth in 1889 and the following entry was identified: *Frederick Raymond Winston, born third quarter 1892, district of Bedminster.* Using his middle initial, together with the information that his wife's name was Hettie, Fred's marriage was found: *Frederick R. Winston married Hetty M. Shortland, second quarter 1922, district of Bristol.* With Hetty's maiden name, it is possible to search for children from the marriage, by entering the surname Winston and the mother's maiden name Shortland. This resulted in two matches: *Donald E. Winston, mother's maiden name Shortland, born second quarter*

1926, district of Bristol and *Joy Winston, mother's maiden name Shortland, born third quarter 1929, district of Bristol.*

Here we have confirmation that the information is correct. We have a Frederick Winston from the Bristol area, married to Hetty, with two children, one called Donald (Donny). Finally, a search for Donny's death found this entry: *Donald Edward Winston, born 15.9.1929, died Feb 2008, district of Gloucester.*

Donald's death certificate confirmed the name and current address of his daughter Belinda, who had registered the death and was in close contact with her Aunt Joy, frail but with a good memory, living in sheltered accommodation in Bristol.

Making an Approach

When you have identified the current details of a relative you have a connection with but have never met, the next step is to make an approach in the hope that they will want to be in touch with you.

You may get only one chance to link up with this relative so it is important to get it right. Contact by telephone should be avoided as an initial method unless you have no other contact information. It is best to make your approach in writing in the first instance (always enclosing an s.a.e. to encourage the contact to respond). You may have found only an email address and perhaps no indication of the area in which your relative lives. If the details were found on a site connected with family history, you are half-way there – this shows that your relative already has an interest and is more likely to respond.

A postal address is likely to be the first way in which you attempt to make contact with a relative. It is important, therefore, to take time gathering and sending the correct information, and above all getting across to your relative that the reason for your approach is genuine.

Family history has become a very popular subject in this country in recent years, but sadly there are some people who are indifferent to genetic links and the heritage of their family. With luck, your research will lead to relatives with whom you can share your interest, but it is possible that their reaction will be lukewarm, or even hostile. Sometimes people can be sceptical or cynical when approached by someone unknown to them, largely due to the hard selling, cold calls and scams that are so widespread.

It should also be pointed out that identity theft has grown rapidly as a method of fraud. Therefore requests for personal information, particularly about names and dates of birth, may be viewed with suspicion. Try to save your questions until later and never request dates of birth and marriage or maiden names, as this information is often used as security questions.

Also, avoid telling someone too much about themselves. Even though many records giving personal information are in the public domain, older people in particular may be unnerved by the fact that someone can find out about them without their knowledge or consent. Some people can also be rather reserved about overt affection or familiar language that might be considered 'forward' or 'gushing'.

Here is an example of a letter that is full of information, and makes no demands:

Dear Mr Coombes

My great-grandfather, George Coombes, born in Nether Walton, Wiltshire, in 1880 had an older brother, James Coombes.

In 1907 George married Alicia Grant (copy of marriage certificate enclosed), and their first son was my grandfather Derek Coombes (1909–1989). My mother, Daphne, is Derek's middle daughter.

We know from census and other public records that James married and had children, including one called Phillip born 1896 in Nether Walton. With the help of a researcher I have learned that you may be a descendant of Phillip Coombes. If so, I would be very happy to hear from you and to share with you the information I have gathered about the Coombes family in Hereford.

I have enclosed details of how to contact me by post, telephone or email and a copy of my draft family tree showing how I think we may be related.

If by any chance I have the wrong Robert Coombes, I am sorry to have troubled you. A short note, email or quick call to let me know would be much appreciated. I have enclosed a self-addressed envelope and first class stamp for your use.

With best wishes,
Diana Bailey (Mrs)

Speculative Letters

Even if you are not certain whether the person you are writing to does have a connection, speculative letters – to all people with the same surname in the right area, for example – can sometimes bring a positive result. A batch of twenty letters can cost less than a few hours of research plus several documents. Taking the trouble to explain your research, print out a chart and enclose document copies may help to encourage a positive response from someone with a family connection.

What to enclose

First of all, a copy of a chart, hand-drawn or computer-generated, showing how you think your families are connected, is most important.

Copies of census returns and certificates that you have acquired during the course of your research could also be included, but not birth certificates relating to the person you are writing to or a member of their immediate family. Indicate clearly on each document what the information relates to, for example, the 1911 census of Nether Walton showing the Coombes family living at 9 Crealey Cottages.

If you wish, you could also include one or two copies of photographs, perhaps one of an ancestor and one of yourself or your family – it can encourage a response if the recipient has a picture of the person they are writing to.

It is always a nice gesture to enclose a self-addressed envelope and at least one postage stamp to cover the reply cost. The Royal Mail website – www.royalmail.com – contains information about addressing envelopes correctly, a search facility for postcodes and an online shop for purchasing postage stamps.

Exchanging Information

Once you have successfully established contact with your relative, you can begin to discover more about their family, exchange information and slowly get to know one another. Do take it

Relationship chart. (© *Karen Bali*)

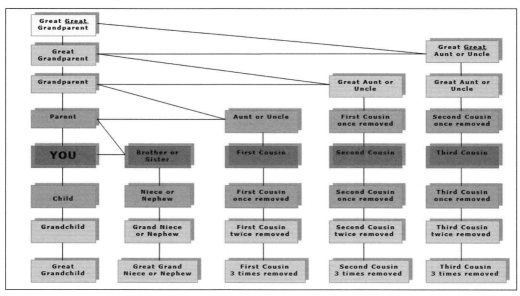

slowly though; don't bombard them with requests for information or pester if they are not quite as quick to reply as you would like.

Working out how you are related to each other is a nice way to break the ice and having a 'third cousin once removed' may be a novelty that your relative is proud to tell everyone about.

Charts like this can help you to work out the name of the relationship between two members within the same extended family. There are also useful good chart and relationship calculators on the following website: www.rhodesfamily.org. uk/people/relationship.html.

DNA Testing

A relatively recent development in the field of family research, DNA testing can not only provide scientific insight into your ancient genetic roots, but also potentially prove a link between individuals going back generations.

Every one of us inherits genetic material from our parents that remains unchanged through the generations, and some of the genes can determine our ancient ancestors or prove connections to distant relatives. The main type of genetic test that is of interest to those researching their family history is for Y chromosome (male) DNA. This tests for DNA that is passed from father to son and remains unchanged through generations, proving genetic links.

There are other types of DNA test, including mitochondrial (female) and autosomal (geographic origins) tests, which are offered by a number of commercial laboratories. Detailed explanations of the science behind these tests and how they can help your research can be found on the following sites, together with information about the cost and procedure:

• **www.oxfordancestors.com** – Professor Bryan Sykes, the founder of Oxford Ancestors, has written several interesting and very readable books. One, about female DNA, is called *The Seven Daughters of Eve*, and another, about male genetics, is called *Adam's Curse: A future without men*. Oxford Ancestors is a laboratory service for genealogy-related DNA testing.

• **www.dnaandfamilyhistory.com** – this website was built to complement a book of the same name by Chris Pomery, *DNA and Family History*, published in 2004 but now out of print. The website contains information about male and female DNA, free downloads and an online order facility for books and DNA testing kits.

• **www.familytreedna.com** – claiming to be the oldest DNA company specifically for genealogy, Family Tree DNA has more than half a million DNA records that can be matched with others from all over the world.

It is important to approach DNA testing with caution, as it may reveal hitherto unsuspected illegitimacy and can potentially cause enormous upset. Unless the newly discovered relatives live in a different county, DNA testing should not be suggested until after you have met and got to know your relatives.

Chapter 12

PRESERVING THE PAST
FOR THE FUTURE

When the time comes to pass on our memories, documents and photographs to a new generation we want to be sure that they will last as long as possible. I spoke with Tony Beardshaw, who runs My History, an established, family-run genealogy supplies company, about the preservation of photographs and documents, and he gave me the following advice.

Firstly, although archivists often wear gloves to handle very old or fragile documents, they can make handling more difficult and accidental tearing more likely. Wash and thoroughly dry your hands before and after handling documents, however, to prevent transfer of bacteria and toxins.

Anything made of paper is naturally acidic and will deteriorate over time, so paper documents need an environment that is as acid-free as possible to ensure that their condition is maintained. Archive boxes, albums and binders can preserve documents for longer. Acid-free polypropylene pockets are best for storing photographs. Do not use the usual A4 clear pockets that can be bought from stationers; they are made of PVC and are not suitable for long-term storage.

Avoid putting original photographs in glass frames. Over time photos can stick to the glass and become damaged. In addition, light can damage photographs so avoid putting them near a window. Don't put photos back to back in albums; even in acid-free pockets the acid in each photo can damage the other. If you stick labels on the back of photographs, use ones that are acid-free and have archive-quality adhesive, as standard adhesive dries out over time and labels fall off.

It goes without saying that documents should not be folded. Do not store original documents in a garage or loft or any environment that can become damp, humid or very cold, and be aware that fluctuating temperatures are very damaging to paper. Fragile, low-quality paper such as newspapers can be very acidic, as they were designed to have a short life. Consider using a neutralising spray to counter the high acid content and prolong the life of this type of document. Clearly label all folders and boxes in which documents and photos are stored so that others can identify the contents if you're not around.

If you must use paperclips, use ones that are made of brass as steel paperclips rust over time and leave stains. Archive-quality boxes and folders only have brass staples that will not rust.

If you want to keep images of your documents and photos, have at least two copies in different formats. CDs can store lots of images but the data is on the surface and vulnerable to damage. External hard drives, in the form of solid state drives (SSD) rather than memory sticks, are a better option.

For more information and details of the wide range of storage products, visit the My History website: www.my-history.co.uk.

When the twenty-first century dawned, the digital age was well under way but still in relative infancy. Today many of us cannot imagine a world before Wikipedia (launched 2001), Facebook (2004) and Twitter (2006), while the global force that is Google had only been around for just over a year (September 1998). In 2000 only around half of the UK population owned a mobile phone. By the end of 2014 the figure was 93 per cent.

We might argue the merits or evils of our reliance on technology, but for the world of genealogy it has opened up countless possibilities, not only for research and connection, but also as an infinite repository for our memories. Just as we can search for genealogical records online from our laptops and instantly connect with relatives worldwide on our smartphones, so we can also create and store documents, pictures, audio, video and family trees.

Free online storage is available with many mainstream email accounts. Outlook (formerly Hotmail), Gmail and Yahoo offer free online space that should be more than adequate for most personal users. Dropbox is a dedicated online storage site with free capacity up to 2GB (as at October 2015). Files, documents, photographs and videos can all be uploaded to these 'cloud-based' accounts that promise safe keeping ad infinitum. Family trees can also be uploaded and shared and not just with your relatives; public trees on Ancestry can be accessed by anyone with an account. Private family trees can be created, grown and shared with chosen individuals for free on Ancestry. Rather than the normal route of accessing the site via the web address, enter http://trees.ancestry.co.uk to start a tree that can only be accessed by you and the relatives you invite to view it.

As always with any virtual product, there is a balance between convenience and security when you choose to upload personal files and information. It is easy to imagine that intangible files on remote servers could be lost, damaged or accidentally deleted. Although this might actually be very unlikely, it can still feel safer to have our photo albums, family Bible and box of letters where we can physically see and handle them. Critics of virtual storage argue that technology can become outdated, companies can fold and hackers can access data that you are led to believe is sitting safely in a virtual cloud. The fact remains that most of the younger generation trust this online home and think nothing of storing their life's memories somewhere that is only accessible through a device with an internet connection.

There is also the question of what happens to all your data once you're no longer around. If accounts can't be accessed without a password, or need periodic re-registration, all of your hard work in scanning, uploading and categorising can go to waste. Whereas a legacy might once have been a treasured possession or the key to a safety deposit box, now it might take the form of login details and permission to perpetuate or deactivate an account that you created. The legal position on virtual ownership and access has only started to become established in recent years and some companies have now formed policies on what happens when account holders die. Google, for example, provides a service called Inactive Account Manager whereby account holders can nominate a trusted person to access an account in the event of extended inactivity. Sharing passwords with close relatives and trusted friends is an option, but not a risk that many would be prepared to take if there were sensitive or financial information to be accessed. Also, it is recommended that different passwords are used for every account and that they are changed regularly, so remembering to update them everywhere is just one more thing to do. One solution is to use a password management service such as 1Password or KeePass to encrypt a file on your computer that contains all of your sensitive information. Another is to save and encrypt a Word document, which is easy to do, although the procedure is slightly different for each version. In Word 2013 use File, Info then Encrypt Document to protect with a password. However, if you forget or lose the password, the document cannot ever be opened. In anticipation of the market to cater for the 'one day to be deceased' online user (which is all of us, after all), a number of companies have set up websites such as Once I've Gone – https://onceivegone.com – on which account holders can specify final wishes, leave farewell messages and store scanned documents. You can read much more about what happens to our online existence when we no longer exist at www.thedigitalbeyond.com or in a book written by Evan Carroll and John

Romano, the founders of that website, *Your Digital Afterlife*. We owe it to ourselves, our children and future generations to preserve memories of the present and the past in as many formats as possible.

REFERENCES AND FURTHER READING

Paul Atterbury, *A life along the line: Railways and People* (David & Charles, 2012)

Karen Bali, *New Cousins: How to Trace Living Descendants of Your Ancestors* (Family History Partnership, 2nd edn, 2012)

Karen Bali, *The People Finder: Reuniting Relatives, Finding Friends* (Nicholas Brealey, 2007)

Gill Blanchard, *Writing Your Family History* (Pen & Sword Books Ltd, 2014)

Evan Carroll and John Romano, *Your Digital Afterlife: When Facebook, Flickr and Twitter Are Your Estate, What's Your Legacy?*, 'Voices That Matter' series (New Riders, 2010)

Census of England and Wales, 1921. Preliminary report including tables of the population enumerated in England and Wales (Administrative and Parliamentary area) and in Scotland, the Isle of Man, and the Channel Islands on 19–20 June 1921 (BPP, 1921, XVI.257). Viewable in full at: www.histpop.org – the Online Historical Population Reports website

Peter Christian, *The Genealogist's Internet* (A&C Black Business Information and Development, 5th rev. edn, 2012)

'Expenditure on the Digitisation of Vital Events project of civil registration records' (Home Office download, 2014)

Janet Few, *The Family Historian's Enquire Within* (Family History Partnership, 6th rev. edn, 2014)

Simon Fowler, *Tracing Your Naval Ancestors: A Guide for Family Historians* (Pen & Sword Family History, 2011)

Simon Fowler, *Tracing Your Army Ancestors: A Guide for Family Historians* (Pen & Sword Family History, 2nd edn, 2013)

Maurice Gorham and Edward Ardizonne, *The Local* (1939; repr. Little Toller 2010)

Emma Jolly, *Tracing Your British Indian Ancestors* (Pen & Sword Family History, 2012)

James McDermott, *British Military Service Tribunals, 1916–1918: 'a very much abused body of men'* (Manchester University Press, 2011)

Arthur Marwickenlarge, *War and Social Change in the Twentieth Century: A Comparative Study of Britain, France, Germany, Russia and the United States* (Palgrave Macmillan, 1974)

Mass Observation, 'The Pub and the People' (an account of the pubs of Bolton) (1938; repr. Faber, 2011)

Heather Norris Nicholson, *Amateur Film: Meaning and Practice, 1927–1977* (Manchester University Press, 2012)

Helen Osborn, *Genealogy: Essential Research Methods* (Robert Hale Ltd, 2012)

Chris Pomery, *Family History in the Genes: Trace Your DNA and Grow Your Family Tree* (National Archives, 2007)

Lesley Richmond and Alison Turton, *The Brewing Industry: A Guide to Historical Records*, Studies in British Business Archives (Manchester University Press, 1990)

Jayne Shrimpton, *Tracing Your Ancestors through Family Photographs: A Complete Guide for Family and Local Historians* (Pen & Sword Family History, 2014)

Lawrence Stone, *Road to Divorce: England 1530–1987* (Oxford University Press, 1990)

Bryan Sykes, *Saxons, Vikings, and Celts: The Genetic Roots of Britain and Ireland* (W.W. Norton & Co., repr. 2008)

Phil Tomaselli, *Tracing Your Air Force Ancestors* (Pen & Sword Family History, 2nd edn, 2014)

Vanessa Toulmin, et al., *The Lost World of Mitchell and Kenyon: Edwardian Britain on Film* (BFI Publishing, 2004)

Nicola Tyrer, *They Fought in the Fields: The Women's Land Army – The Story of a Forgotten Army* (Mandarin, 1997)

Simon Wills, *Tracing Your Merchant Navy Ancestors* (Pen & Sword Family History, 2012)

Geoffrey Yeo, *The British Overseas: A Guide to Records of Their Births, Baptisms, Marriages, Deaths and Burials, Available in the United Kingdom* (Guildhall Library Research Guides, 3rd edn, 1995)

'The Lost World Of Mitchell And Kenyon': Complete BBC Series [DVD] (2004)

'Tracing Great War Ancestors: Finding Uncle Bill' [DVD] (Pen & Sword Digital, 2010)

INDEX